YOUR VOICE YOUR CHOICE

A STORY of RESILIENCY & REDEMPTION

by APRIL HERNANDEZ CASTILLO

The CoolSpeak Publishing Company

Cover Photo by Joel Grimes
Born in the Bronx Picture by Joe Conzo Jr.
Cover design and Photo Touch Up - Rick Navarro

Book design by Carlos Ojeda Jr. and CoolSpeak Publishing
Company.

Cover design by Carlos Ojeda Jr.

ISBN-13: **978-0692521304**

What People Are Saying About
Your Voice, Your Choice

Erika Alexander
Actress Living Single, writer Concrete Park: August 2015

"April Hernandez Castillo is beautiful, funny, strong, confident and successful. She is a movie star, a TV host, a wife and a mother. April Hernandez Castillo is also a survivor of Intimate Partner Violence. Her journey from wounded young woman to motivational speaker and domestic violence advocate takes us down a dark road into the light of self-discovery and spiritual growth.

As a friend, it was hard for me to read her story; she suffered years of degradation and humiliation. I was disturbed to discover that the strong young woman I knew could ever have endured that type of oppression. The warrior that emerges in these pages is more profound and bright than the world could have created without that pain. The April she became is fiercely talented and dedicated to the empowerment of woman and girls.

In a world full of reality TV and selfies, April stands a woman apart, unafraid to explore the lies and truth of what it is to be human. She is an unashamedly spiritual and unapologetically worldly woman. She challenges you to get up and make something happen. April Hernandez Castillo is a star. April Hernandez is the future."

Rita Smith
Consultant to the National Football League and national expert on violence against women.

"I met April Hernandez while I was the director of the National Coalition Against Domestic Violence. She was a keynote speaker at the NCADV conference in 2012, her message was powerful and brought the entire crowd to their feet.

This book continues to build on her effort to educate others. It provides two powerful components, the first is the reality that while every victim of abuse is unique, their experiences are eerily similar, no matter who they are or where they live. The second critical component is the great gift that April's story gives us, the ability to more fully understand the impact of the violence on her and by extension others, and the incredible ability of those abused to recover and thrive once they find the support they need to leave the violence."

Dedication

"No, in all these things we are more than conquerors through him who loved us." - Romans 8:37 (NIV)

I dedicate this book to the YOU, the reader. I have dreamt of writing a book for over 15 years and the fact I get to share such a personal story with you means the world to me. You are a part of a dream that once seemed so far away. The physical abuse I endured almost ended my life, but today I stand as a woman who conquered and persevered. My hope is once you have finished reading this book a fire will be ignited inside of you to look at any situation and say despite my reality it is not my destiny. You have the power to make a choice today to live a life where your voice matters and to speak up when you see something. So, what are you waiting for?

Contents

Foreword

Two years ago I was asked to host a television show that was going to be syndicated across the country. I know TV is something God has called me to do with my life, so when the offer was made, I took it, despite the fact that it paid so little I'm embarrassed to give you the actual figure. Let's just say it was in the very low four digits in the base ten number system.

Also, I've always felt that I had what you might call an evening TV persona, and this was very much a morning show. Still, I thought it might be fun to try. I also thought that I would learn some things about TV and it might develop into something else eventually. It didn't. It also wasn't syndicated or picked up on any TV stations of which I'm aware. Not that it matters, because a true artist doesn't do television to please some audience. He does it for himself. Okay, I'm kidding. If there's no audience, what's the point? So we taped twenty-six episodes and I have no idea who has seen them. I also was sure we would continue taping a second season. We didn't. I forgot to mention that I never wanted to do a show with a co-host, and this show had a co-host. Her name was April Hernandez Castillo.

I knew virtually nothing about April except that she was an actress and a Latina. But so are Chita Rivera and Carmen Miranda. But sometimes you just go with it and see what God has in store. And meeting April ended up being wonderful. Why do I say that? Because she asked me to. Okay, I'm kidding again. I say that it was wonderful because it really was wonderful. And it was wonderful because April is someone I quickly realized was a person of real substance. She had not had it easy in her life, but she had a great attitude. And that's because her faith was rock solid. I realized that she wasn't a "Christian". She was a Christian. She took her faith seriously and she wasn't afraid to talk about it and be in your face about it, if necessary. This is somewhat rare among actresses who have starred in *bona fide* movies, which she has. April was also feisty, which is actually *not* rare among Latinas from the Bronx, and I particularly enjoyed that about her. And she was genuinely funny, which really is rare. Very few people can crack me up, and April could and did, many times. So we had a lot of fun taping all those episodes together. By the way, did I mention the show was never syndicated as promised? I did? Well, that's because it wasn't syndicated as promised. But as I say, we had fun, and more importantly, I made a real friend. His name was Howard. Just kidding! Of course I'm talking about April.

I almost forgot to say that one day on the way home from our TV gig — it was taped in a foreign country that rhymes with Canada — I asked April a question I've asked many of my friends in the last few years. I asked her if she had ever experienced a real miracle. I was writing a book on miracles and wanted to include the miracle stories of people I know. April was silent for a moment. And then she said that yes, she had. And then she told me an extraordinary story. It was so extraordinary that I put it in my book on miracles, which is titled *Miracles*. And when I got my radio show I had her on to tell the story to a wider audience. As I knew when we were taping it, it was a story that would affect many lives. There are so many women who have been through things similar to April, and her faith and her boldness and her authenticity in telling her stories gives those other women strength. Just as the stories she tells in this book will do. When someone is funny and authentic and serious about their faith and their troubles, you really should listen. Because it will bless you. So that's what Your Voice, Your Choice is about and I hope you will enjoy it and be inspired by it. If you're not, you might be reading the wrong book. Please check the title and try again.

Eric Metaxas
New York Times Best Selling Author-Bonhoeffer: Pastor, Martyr, Prophet, Spy

Born In The Bronx

Whenever I have traveled out of NYC and someone asks me where I'm from, I proudly reply "I was born and raised in the Bronx." Then I proceed to ask them, what do they know about the Bronx? And I am usually met with these words- the Yankees or Jennifer Lopez. Now as much as I appreciate JLO for all of her accomplishments and being from the Bronx - it's sort of a birth right to be a Yankee fan especially being a Puerto Rican from the Bronx- we love the Yankees with all our heart and soul. In 1996, I was sixteen years old, and the Yankees were in the World Series playing against the Atlanta Braves. They had not won a World Series since 1978, so the anticipation was at an all- time high and they were also playing at the home field in the Bronx which added more drama to this intense game. At the time, George Steinbrenner and Joe Torre were running the team which in my opinion was one of the best ever as for my generation. They were referred to as the *Dynasty team* with players such as Derek Jeter, Wade Boggs, Bernie Williams, and my favorite player of all time- Paul O Neil. I remember that night like if it were yesterday; my father, brother Phillip, and myself up late sitting on the edge of our seats like little children awaiting Santa Clause to come through the chimney (although there were no chimneys in the Bronx, we had fire escapes.) The excitement and anticipation was just so electrifying because the Yankees were playing in the Bronx and on their home field. The sounds of screaming fans crept through the open windows and hallway doors, as every other family in the Bronx watched the game as though we were all one big happy family.

Now my father, who had loved the Yankees since being in his mother's womb, preferred to use a particular whistle (which by the way is one of the most annoying whistles I have ever heard) and every time he blew on it, he implied the Yankees were close to winning. My mother on the other hand, had no interest in watching the game with us. When she would pass by to go to the kitchen, she would make these outlandish statements while flaring her nose.

"Aye, those Yankees are going to lose like they always do." I made sure my dad would blow the whistle obnoxiously louder because we knew it would get under her skin.

As the game got closer to the end, I was sweating and jumping on my brother while the whistle was going off like a siren, and then it happened- the Yankees won! The entire stadium went up in up roar of excitement; people were hugging each other and celebrating as if they won themselves. My father, brother and I screamed as well and went outside to celebrate with the guys from the neighborhood. I truly believe the Yankees winning the World Series gave us a sense of pride like never before along with major bragging rights. I was so proud to be from the Bronx. But there was a time if you even mentioned the word the Bronx it would be met with judgment and frowned down upon.

"Ladies and Gentlemen, The Bronx is burning." A quote, attributed to Howard Cosell on October 12th, 1977, had been around long before Game 2 of the 1977 World Series. In fact, devastation in the Bronx was so widespread by the day that those words reached households across America, one week before; President Jimmy Carter made a visit to the Bronx. As his motorcade drove through the streets, making a stop on Charlotte Street, the residents who noticed his fanfare screamed at him, begging for jobs, help, food and security. Even President Reagan after making a visit one time compared it to "London after the blitz".

In the 1960's, desegregation was on the rise and the government in the South Bronx started coming up with its own way of supporting racial bias. As the city government failed in their attempt to follow suit with the rest of the United States, people began to leave the Bronx. In ten years, the population in the Bronx dropped by 57%. As residents disappeared and landlords were left without tenants, they began to either let the buildings they owned deteriorate so badly that the electrical system's caught fire, or purposely set the buildings on fire so they could collect their insurance money and abandon the city just like the others already had.

But that night, as a helicopter's camera caught the image of a burning building just blocks from Yankee stadium, people across America thought they were seeing the beginning of something electric in the Bronx. America had no idea the streets of the Bronx had been on fire for years and would slowly burn more.

I was born into the flames.

I came into a world where it was hard to tell the difference between snowflakes and ashes. I never saw a reason to. Both were beautiful in my world. *My world.*

My mother, Maria Alvarado, gave birth to me on January 31st 1980 in Jacobi hospital via C-section. I was breached and the doctors were doing everything they could to straighten me out, but in the end C-section was the only option left. She always says how I waited till the last day of the coldest month to make an entrance to the world. Maria decided to name me April, which has always been interesting to me because I was born in January and not many Puerto Ricans, especially in those days, named their daughters April. There were basically two choices, Maria or Sandra, but never an April. My stomping grounds would be 179th street between Creston and the Grand Concourse. Now, before I was born, the building my parents moved into was predominantly Jewish and was actually considered to be an upper class neighborhood. My parents, along with one other lady, were the only

Puerto Ricans in the building, which I am sure, did not go so well due to racial tensions. Eventually, as the Bronx continued to burn and the poverty level rose, the Jewish people departed and the apartments became occupied with primarily blacks and Latinos.

As I reflect back and reminisce, I can't find the ugliness so many people refer to when they talk about the Bronx in the 1980's. As the fires died down, another kind of inferno began to rule the streets. *Crack*.

Better known as the Crack epidemic era.

I don't remember a time I didn't know what crack was. I knew from growing up in the streets, listening to my parents, and Ronald Regan who was president at the time began waging a war against drugs. *Crack is Wack*. One of the most infamous phrases New Yorkers would hear throughout the 80's. By the time I was eight I'd seen my share of creepy crack heads on the streets and that was enough to scare me away from any curiosity that might've entered my mind. It was impossible to walk down the streets without finding at least ten crack vials on any given day. I could have picked a bouquet of crack vials more easily than one of daisies. And I did. Life wasn't this picture perfect fairytale full of green grass and sandboxes, but I didn't know those things even existed, I knew the Bronx and I was completely happy.

For the most part, I had my run of the streets of the Bronx and I knew how far was too far. When summertime came, time stopped. Days and nights melted together and my world was perfect. I'd stop in for a meal at home, sometimes I'd bring a friend along, and we'd head back out on another adventure. The buildings on our block were so tall that I'd have to lie on the ground to be able to see all the way to the top of them and they were lined up as far as my eyes could see. They guarded me as I explored all of them and there was never a time I can remember being scared. In fact, I can still see the face of a woman lit up by nothing but the moonlight, walking towards me like a zombie and asking me, an eight-year-old child, if I had any crack. It may have been midnight or later, but the woman had no concern for a child wandering the streets after dark and I had no concern a crack-addicted woman was trying to talk to me. I'd simply say no and she'd say something like, "Okay, thank you." Even the crack heads were polite. I remained unfazed by the irony of it all. If you don't know anything else exists, you don't wish for anything else. I knew what blocks I could travel to and the ones I had to stray away from. But my block from 179th street and Grand Concourse to Creston Avenue was the safe haven.

I'd gather together my group of friends, and we made our block our playground. There was one building in particular which served as a clubhouse of sorts for us. We'd kept it a secret for the most part, securely known by only our small group of friends, specifically because it had one amazing amenity that the other buildings did not have.

A mattress.

No, not for sleeping or laying on, but a mattress specifically for jumping! I can remember my hair flying in front of my eyes, splashing on my face because it was drenched in sweat as I catapulted into the air like I was gliding in slow motion just like an Olympian. I can see the smiles on the faces of the kids I grew up with and I can feel the comfort and fearlessness I had, knowing that right then, nothing could possibly hurt me. I knew the mattress would catch me when I flipped back. In the middle of all the rubbish was my oasis and it was perfect.

Getting to the mattress was an adventure in itself. Seems to me, when I remember, everything in the Bronx was broken. But this particular area seemed to have more broken glass than anything. We had to walk through the glass to get to the mattress, which was almost as much fun as jumping on the mattress itself and actually quite dangerous as I come to think about it. Plus, I was always pretty competitive as a young girl and desired to be the best when it came to running through copious amounts of broken beer bottles without falling. The whole area was a junkyard and as you flew up and down in the air, you could see the clouds pass by overhead and the array of broken junk around us was our own personal kaleidoscope. No one ever even thought about the other activities that might've taken place on the mattress when we weren't around, I mean, who would? Paradise was there in front of us and there was no way we were going to analyze the situation. It was time to jump! We could fly into the sky and around us was a whirlwind of colors and light. Suddenly, all of the things that were broken, the glass and the trash, were beautiful. As a child, I don't know that I remember seeing anything more spectacular.

Well, maybe one thing, fireworks. If you aren't from the city then you might not understand this, but there was nothing like the Fourth of July in the Bronx. Humidity hovered over the streets and my hair was always some sort of insane, but I loved it. I have always loved everything about it. The anticipation of the Fourth of July in my neighborhood created this sense of community which unfortunately is nonexistent these days. Day to day we always helped one another out. We protected each other and stood up for one another. But on the Fourth, everyone was together, outside, while music was blasting ranging from a selection of Salsa to Hip Hop. No matter what the weather was like or how much crime was happening on the streets on the fourth, none of the terrible things that everyone knows or thinks they know about the Bronx existed. All that existed was family. The mothers of my friends would cook rice, beans, and chicken and I would hurriedly run to the store and buy my favorite soda, *Cola Champagne,* to go with my meal. Everyone had a sparkler to share and the fireworks appeared as though they were surely going to set the Bronx on fire once again. But they never did. They died out and so did the camaraderie.

Somewhere along the way the community I grew to love on Creston Avenue realized it was broken and people stopped caring. The children grew into teenagers and the Fourth of July just became another monotonous holiday. I have always vowed that I will see my city come to life again in a positive light. God has not abandoned the Bronx, but instead he has chosen it and those who live there are destined for greatness.

So, I went on, growing up in the streets. When the 1990's arrived Hip Hop had shifted into a more aggressive flow. Girls wore baggy jeans and oversized shirts with Timberland boots. Women were becoming more independent and really finding their voices. The era of the stay at home mom was slowly diminishing and artists like Madonna, TLC, and Salt & Peppa were talking more about sex. I wasn't afraid to say what I needed to say when I needed to say it and to whomever I thought needed to hear it at any time. Being born in the Bronx, especially during the crack epidemic era, you had to be tough because it was a means of survival. Needless to say, I was a tomboy and I wasn't going to let anyone push me around. All of my best friends were boys, so when I did say too much, I wasn't scared because I knew I had them to stand up for me. I was absolutely fearless. Really I was. I pretty much walked the streets late at night and never felt afraid. One of my friend's mothers could not believe I was going to be walking home at two o' clock in the morning and begged me to stay over but I kind of felt invisible and knew I would be ok. Oddly enough if I happen to stay out late these days you can catch me running to my building for safety.

I can't really say I was a rebellious teenager who immaturely disobeyed my parents. I did not go around picking fights with girls just for the heck of it but that did not mean I escaped fights either. There was a girl in my class named Blossom and believe me she did not personify her name. I'm not sure why Blossom didn't like me. A lot of the kids that I knew were jealous of me and my brother because we were blessed enough to have both of our parents. My father was kind and generous and it was very clear to everyone he was a good man. The people in my neighborhood also knew he was a crazy Puerto Rican who loved and protected his family; he was a hero to many of them just as he was my hero. I cannot remember ever taking a breath at a time where I didn't know that my father loved me more than he loved himself. My mother was a feisty beautiful Puerto Rican mother who was stern in her ways and wanted both my brother and I to be great in life. Most of my friends had only one parent because the other was either addicted to drugs, dead or missing. Others lived with their grandparents or another family member because both of their parents were gone. I was blessed to have grown up in a loving, happy, traditional family.

Eventually, Blossom called me out in the hallway and asked me if I knew how to fight. I was really blown away because I had no idea why she would even ask me that question. I told her "No" I didn't know how to fight and I walked away. I thought it was the end of it, but later at lunch, Blossom charged me. I honestly didn't know how to react when it happened. There I was, being pushed by this girl for no apparent reason, and I froze. That lasted about three seconds.

Before I even knew what I was doing, my instincts kicked in and I fought back. I really can't remember exactly what the fight was like, I just remember feeling, that fight or flight, get out of there or get ready to fight back feeling. My face got hot and my heartbeat was noticeable, pounding in my throat, and boom, I was fighting for the first time in my life. The survival instincts which roared inside of me took over and I was going to do one thing: *survive*. The next thing I remember is sitting in the principal's office wondering how I even got there. I still had no idea why this girl wanted to fight me in the first place. All I knew was that when she put the pressure on, I had no control over my fight or flight response. I was not going to let anyone push me around, not then, not ever. I did not want my friends to think I was a punk. I might have lost control, but I consciously made the choice in that moment no one was going to bully me again.

Later in life I had no idea I would be fighting a bigger fight- *Teen Dating Violence*. I had never been exposed to any kind of abuse or domestic violence in my household. My mother always reminded me to be myself and never ever allow anyone to take my voice away, but we never discussed the situations where it could happen. I don't think anyone ever predicted there was a possibility of anyone taking advantage of the spunky little Puerto Rican girl from 179th street and Creston. I mean I was the girl who would tell her friends if a guy ever put his hands on me I would fight back! I wanted to be Cheetara from the greatest cartoon ever –*The Thunder Cats*. I was a big dreamer. I was destined for greatness. But the abuse did happen and it happened in a way where shame completely took over my soul and silenced my voice. The girl who fearlessly wandered the streets of the burning Bronx at 2am looking for another adventure existed no more. Even at the present moment writing these words I know there is a teenage girl, a woman, a child and even a man who has experienced such pain and trauma because of abuse. Somewhere along the way abuse has silenced their voices and they may feel as if they have no choices in life.

Have you lost your voice or forgotten what life was like when you were a child? Do you remember a moment that defined the voice you knew lived inside of you? Do you remember the second someone deafened your ears to the sound of that voice? Was there a choice that had to be made?

Maybe you still hear a little bit of the voice inside of yourself and you think that you can find it again. It's your choice if that voice stays silent or screams. Take a moment to remember what your childhood was like, even if it was difficult. Find a memory, even if you have only one, and meditate on it for a minute. Remember what it felt like to be happy, even if the sad times are trying to flood your mind. Maybe you are thinking that you don't have one happy memory at all. But let me tell you something, God has a memory of you and it's not the one that you have. His memory of you isn't dark and damaged. He sees a bright, shining light of existence standing in the middle of the darkness. He created you with a purpose and a voice that can conquer every negative thought inside of your head.

You are beautiful. You are perfect. You were created for more than the darkness.

Now it's time for you to make a choice. It's your voice and it's your choice. Find your voice. Find one thing, even if it's the smallest hobby like running or painting, and pour your voice into it. You don't have to change all at once and let me tell you, it took me a very long time to find my voice once I lost it. But you have to start somewhere. Choose one thing that makes you feel like you are being heard and be passionate about it. Choose to listen to your voice today and tomorrow will be a little bit brighter.

Born In The Bronx
Your Voice, Your Choice

- Describe a childhood memory that has had a huge impact on your life.

  _____

  _____

  _____

  _____

  _____

- What were some lessons you learned while growing up that you still live by till this day?

  _____

  _____

  _____

  _____

  _____

- If there was one thing you could do differently what would it be and why?

  _____

  _____

  _____

  _____

  _____

  _____

  _____

  _____

Your Reality Is Not Your Destiny

Eventually the Bronx stopped burning but the drugs remained rampant on the streets. I remember when the movie *New Jack City* made its debut in theaters, I was blown away at how accurate the film mirrored the severity of crack and how it not only took over the Bronx but NYC as a whole. Wesley Snipes, who happens to be a *Bronxite* himself- a Bronx native, was playing the ruthless and heartless drug dealer, Nino Brown. Snipes character utilized abandoned buildings to build his crack empire and was willing to rise to power by any means necessary; even if it meant killing his best friend G Money. But I did not have to watch the movie to witness first hand buildings being used for drug business because I was surrounded by them not to far from where I lived. That was my reality and unlike Nino Brown, who murdered his right hand man, I had a best friend and her name was, Q.

We lived in a different reality. Nothing could hurt us and together we could accomplish anything. Together, we were Q & A. The dynamic duo, double trouble, two of a kind; it was us against the world. She would ask the question and I would give the answer. But like I said, our world was small and as long as we kept it that way, we knew we'd always be together. But as you know, free spirits and open minds die if they are smothered, and just like the flames that blazed across the Bronx we'd both eventually have to come to the realization, if we wanted to stay on fire, we'd have to find somewhere else to burn. Our little world would never be big enough for both of us.

The buildings in my neighborhood were stacked like dominos standing in a line waiting to get knocked over. Q lived in the building directly across from mine. (This was a huge blessing.) You see, back in my day before the world of the internet and cell phones, we had to actually use a house phone; a rotary phone at that. I know it is hard to believe we had to physically dial a number one at a time in a circular motion but it worked. Another way Q and I communicated was calling each other out our windows, especially if the phone had been cut off due to our parents not making payments. Q would pop her head out the window and we would talk about what was on the agenda for the day and give a time to meet outside. My parents still live where I grew up and sometimes I find myself looking out the window to where Q lived. The little girl inside wants to scream for Q's name but I think the neighbors would think I am a little crazy. So I just stare and reminisce.

In fact, getting to Q's apartment was always an adventure you see she lived on the 5th floor and there was no elevator. That was a curse. As an adult, I love to exercise and stay in shape. Back then, I was pulling off a workout that would have ruined the biggest Crossfit stud you've ever seen, and I was doing it several times a day. Up five flights and down five flights, high fives and butterflies, back and forth and up and down, neither of us seemed to notice a strain at all. A strong slap on the top of the banister as I turned the corner to start on the next flight would echo all the way back down to the ground level on a good day. Once in a while it was too loud and random doors would open and dirty looks from tired residents would pierce my eyes and just inspire me to run faster and to be stronger. I started to love to run because that meant I got to be with Q. On a good day, I'd even skip steps and see how fast I could go. It could have been one hundred degrees outside and I never would have noticed a difference. We were together and it was fun and perfect. We were the magnificent Q & A. Eventually, I'd run up and down those stairs so many times that people quit peeking out to see what all of the commotion was. They knew.

Since I was the only girl in my family, Q was more than a best friend she was a sister to me. We spent so much time together that we'd finish each other's sentences. She was raised by her grandmother and it wasn't long before Q's family took me in and saw me as family. I would refer to her grandmother as my own. She'd feed me rice and beans on a regular basis. It was delicious and no matter how many times I've tried to replicate the taste of her recipe, I just can't.

While the rice was boiling on the stove though, I only have to take one deep breath and I'm back in her kitchen waiting for lunch. I can see Q smiling at me and hear her grandmother mumbling about something we'd gotten into as she stirred the rice in the boiling water.

Our wardrobes began to intertwine and eventually we couldn't even remember which outfit belonged to which girl in the first place. Q always had such a great sense of style and because she was a few years older than me I would want to wear everything she wore. Asics, which is a well-established sneaker brand company, were one of our favorites to wear. Particularly, we loved the pair that had the colors orange and purple. Q and I would make sure if we wore those sneakers that our outfits matched perfectly. My mother would always tell me "Just because you are poor doesn't mean you have to look poor." I guess she was right because when Q and A hit the streets all of our friends would comment and say how cool we looked. We also had to match the sneakers with our Champion t shirts. We couldn't afford the official ones so we purchased the shirts on the streets for five dollars. The only thing about buying the imitation Champion shirts is that after washing them in the washing machine, the letters began to peel off which was so not cool for us. So, the shirts had to be hand washed. Everyone in the neighborhood also knew that if you saw Q; A wasn't far behind.

I never really thought about it when I was a child, but I'm sure God put us together because we needed each other, and there were days when I did realize how much Q needed me. There were occasions when her mother and father would show up out of the blue and for a fleeting moment, you could see the light in her eyes grow brighter. She had hoped that maybe this time her parents were finally going to stay. But they never stayed. Both Q's mother and father were addicted to the one thing that dominated the streets of the Bronx. Crack.

When Q's parents did come around, I'd try and back off and let her spend time with them. I knew from my experience with my parents how important it was for a young lady yearning for the attention of a parent. I had two great parents who loved me unconditionally. I had a father who was present at all times. Actually my parents loved Q very much and knew of her situation and would always encourage her to dream big and go to college one day. But still, if it is not coming from your own parents it can't really fill the void in one's heart.

It was a typical hot and humid summer day in the Bronx, and Q and I, had just finished playing a game of basketball. We started walking home and talking about ways we could make money. I thought I could do some cleaning, maybe help one of the older ladies hang her laundry or run to the market and pick up some groceries for someone.

Q looked at me and said, "I think I could sell crack."

There was a long pause on my end. My head was spinning a mile a minute. I could not digest what she had just revealed. Let me tell you something about Puerto Rican women. When we don't like something, it's almost impossible for us to avoid making a face that obviously shows how much we dislike whatever that something is. In that moment, I'm sure she recognized the look on my face and she quickly recovered her thoughts and said, "You can't tell anyone. You have to swear." She looked down at her long skinny legs and pulled the curls out of her face. She was nervous, but she trusted me. She looked up at me with her big black eyes and said it again. "You have to swear."

I swore of course, because that's what best friends do. Q went on to reveal to me that when her mother did come and see her, she'd take her along with her to the crack houses. Most of the time, her mother would leave her in a room and go off to get high. The room was usually the place where the crack was being prepared. She'd watch the dealers cut it and package it, weigh it and cut it again. She explained every detail to me about how to make crack and how she could make enough money from it to get out of the Bronx. Maybe even stay out. Crack could save her. That was her reality.

In my heart, I cried for Q. I didn't know the word back then but I knew what it meant to be pretentious and I couldn't behave that way towards my best friend. I had a loving family; no one I knew directly was addicted to drugs. My mother was home every night when I went to sleep and there was always food waiting for me to eat it. My father made jokes with me and repeatedly told me I was beautiful and perfect every chance he got. My life was pretty okay.

Q's grandmother was not only raising her but her sister and a cousin. She did the best she could with what she had. Unfortunately, her mother and father loved being high more than they loved being with her at the time. Her life was not easy. Her world was not peaceful. Her reality was defining her life, and bit by bit, pieces of her were being sucked in to the black hole of that reality and she was losing the light that used to show up in her eyes.

But I was taught to dream big. I was taught to never give up. And I wasn't going to give up on my best friend; that was for sure. As we started to go from scrawny little girls to developing teenagers, we also started to see our world from two different sets of eyes. As I mentioned, Q was a few years older than me so naturally we slowly grew apart. She was ready to grow up much faster than I was. She was excited about boys. I mean why wouldn't she be? I wasn't allowed to have a boyfriend although most of my friends were boys. But when she realized that having a boyfriend could fill that void, I couldn't compete. My love for her had gotten her to this point in her life, but it was no longer enough. I couldn't push anymore and she didn't want me to. She was done with Q and A and my heart was broken.

One of the fondest memories I have of us as teenagers, before we began to drift as friends, was at a jam (also known as a party). I don't even really remember who invited us to the party but it was in a neighborhood we rarely visited. These jams would be held in someone's house and sometimes we would have to pay five dollars to get in. Q was annoyed with me because I kept saying that I didn't feel comfortable and something was fishy. It was really dark in the apartment and people were smoking and drinking. It just didn't feel safe. So much so that Q finally agreed to leave with me. We have a tendency as human beings to not listen to our instincts but we should because most of the time its right. It is our spirit revealing something before it happens.

We finally decided to leave. When we started going down the stairs we heard a commotion and jetted out the building. While we were standing outside in front of the building a man a few feet away from me pulled out a gun pointed to the sky and shot off some rounds.

Our instincts kicked in and both of us started to run. Just like those days on the staircase, skipping steps and slapping the banister, we were running. Like Forrest Gump.

"Are you shot?" I screamed as we ran. "Are you shot? Are you shot?" The streets were black and dark and we kept running and running. I don't know how no one noticed. I don't understand how no one asked if we were okay. But I also don't remember seeing anyone or anything but the darkness as we ran through the streets. I'm not sure why we decided to stop or if our bodies simply could not go anymore, but we eventually did and in that moment we simultaneously started laughing and crying. We were both okay. We weren't shot. We stood staring at one another, two girls from the same block with matching black eyes and curly hair, two pairs of identical skinny legs and warm smiles that looked like a reflection in a mirror. I went home that night and laid in my bed thanking God neither of us were harmed. I don't think I could have lived with myself if something did happen to Q. Her grandmother would always tell me I had to keep her safe. I did. I miss Q very much but eventually our worlds would part.

Like any relationship, losing Q left me scarred. I began to try and make more friends, but I was guarded. When the cool kids at my school invited me to be a part of their group, I was pumped. If I didn't have a best friend anymore, at least the cool kids liked me. My parents gave me a lot of freedom to make my own mistakes, and for the most part I stayed on the straight and narrow. I knew my boundaries and I was always open and honest with them. I was one of the lucky ones. I didn't want to be rebellious. In addition to my parents, I had a teacher that had a huge impact on my life. His name was Mr. Rasul and he came along right at a time when I needed someone special in my world. I'd lost Q and I was trying to figure out who I was without Q and A.

As a teenager with loving parents, I often assumed that my parents had no choice but to love me, to believe in me. But Mr. Rasul was different from other teachers. First off, he was a Black Muslim teaching in a catholic school. So go figure. But I can still remember Mr. Rasul telling my father how special I was at a parent teacher conference. I soaked it up. "That girl is going to be somebody someday. She's going to change the world." Mr. Rasul challenged us as students to dream beyond our realities. I have never been able to find Mr. Rasul after I graduated. I hope to find him one day and thank him for his words of wisdom, love, and hope.

I believed Mr. Rasul because he believed in me. The realities set before me were saying there was no way this tomboy from the Bronx would ever change anything in the world. But the words of one caring man made me believe in a bigger destiny for myself. I wanted to do great, to be great, to be more than what everyone thought I could be. I had big dreams for me and Q. We were supposed to conquer the world together. Unfortunately, it didn't happen.

Years later I reunited with Q. We were now women whose lives had taken two completely different roads than what we set out for as kids. I was finally able to ask her where did our friendship go wrong? Q emotionally revealed she had been jealous of me for years. Jealous I had the family she always wanted, jealous of how much I had going for myself and it just became too much for her to handle. We cried. We hugged. We closed that chapter in our lives. Sure, I was born into different circumstances than Q but my life has not been perfect. It is amazing as I think about the friendship we had because I thought I knew everything about Q. I was sure we would be together forever. But the reality was we would travel down different roads of our lives as women. Losing a friendship can be devastating especially when you find it difficult to trust people. It took many years for me to allow someone back into my life after my friendship with Q.

One of the biggest issues I hear most of the time especially from the youth is dealing with trust issues. Has someone you loved violated your trust in such a way you have closed off your heart? Have you ever said "I don't really trust people like that"? Especially if you have been violated sexually, physically, mentally, and emotionally being able to trust anyone can seem so far away. When I fell in love with my abuser I trusted him with my heart and soul. I gave him a part of my heart no man ever possessed. Only my daddy had that kind of access to my heart because he was the one who taught me how a man should love a woman. So giving my all to my ex-boyfriend was a natural progression. But the moment my trust was broken after the first time he laid hands on me, a part of me slowly began to die.

Can I promise you that you will never get hurt again in life? No, I can't. Can I promise you that life will be easy and beautiful all the time? No, I can't. This is not a self-help book where you will say five affirmations a day and your life will turn out great. I am sorry if I disappointed you but I don't have the time to waste to play nice with you. Your time is valuable to me and my desire is you will get to a place of loving and trusting again. This book was created to get you to a place where you look deep within yourself and begin to do the work no matter what age or gender you are.

Now I am telling you, **YOU** are enough. **YOU** are powerful. **YOU** were created for a purpose. Don't allow anyone to tell you otherwise. It doesn't matter where you live, what you were born into, or who is telling you otherwise; your reality is not your destiny. Your surroundings do not dictate who you are or who you will be. It's your voice! You have a choice. What will you choose today? Do you choose to accept your reality as it is? Or will you let your voice be heard and embrace your destiny?

Today is a day that you will never get back. You only get one shot at living today so go for it! You might be young and wild, but you are smart and talented and can find a place in this world that was made just for you.

Your Reality Is Not Your Destiny
Your Voice, Your Choice

- What is the reality of your life today?

  _____
  _____
  _____
  _____
  _____
  _____

- Are there any changes you can begin to implement today in order to reach your destiny?

  _____
  _____
  _____
  _____
  _____
  _____

- What do you believe is your destiny?

  _____
  _____
  _____
  _____
  _____
  _____
  _____

Your Voice Is Powerful

"No... wire... hangers. What's wire hangers doing in this closet when I told you: no wire hangers EVER?"

These words may sound crazy, but they represent one of my fondest childhood memories of being with my mother as we would watch the movie, *Mommy Dearest* together. Faye Dunaway's portrayal of Hollywood actress Joan Crawford, marked my life forever. Her perfectly lined lips and vehement hostility towards her daughter Christina, did not frighten me. I wasn't scared of her. I admired her because she was a fiercely beautiful woman with a tough streak, just like my own mother.

I admired my mother. She's never really been the kind of woman to be quite loquacious. As a matter of fact, her- facial expressions did more talking than anything else, especially when my brother and I would get reprimanded. My mother would make a certain gesture when she wanted to get her point across to us that she was serious. She would flare her nostrils and raise her right eyebrow just like Dwayne "The Rock" Johnson would do in a wrestling match. We automatically knew we had better stop misbehaving, or else there would have been some pretty serious consequences.

My mother, Maria Alvarado, was born in May of 1952 in the beautiful town of Gurabo, Puerto Rico. Also known as, "La Ciudad de las Escaleras," which means "city of stairs," the center of Gurabo has a vivid staircase that looks like it is climbing up to heaven. But Gurabo was no heaven for Maria Alvarado. Being raised by a single mother doing her best to provide for her five children would prove to be a difficult task.

"We were so poor we couldn't even afford shampoo and forget about conditioner. My mother washed my hair with bath soap and nothing else. We did what we had to do to make things work."

I can't even begin to imagine my mother attempting to wash my hair with only bar soap; I would probably come out looking like Simba from the Lion King.

One of my other favorite things to hear my mother talk about when she has opened up about her life is when she met my father. When they started dating she would tell my father, "I like you because nobody knows who you are."

To this day my father says that comment was comical because on the streets, there wasn't anybody who didn't know who he was. This blew my mother's mind. She was more of an introvert and my dad was the guy in the neighborhood everyone knew and loved. Before meeting my mother, his two loves in life were stick ball and salsa.

Their romance was a whirlwind and they moved in with each other rather quickly. My father says he knew she was the one the moment he saw her, but if you ask my mother, her side of the story sounds something like this:

"I needed a place to live and he offered and I said yes. We never thought we would last this long together." (They have been married for over 40 years.)

Both my parents have had very difficult lives but they knew when they decided to build a family they would do everything in their power to give us the world. And they did. Christmas was my favorite holiday because my mom made the house feel like Rockerfeller Center. Lights flooded the apartment while Christmas carols played all night long and the smell of my mother's rice and beans permeated every crevice. "The Christmas Song" by Nat king Cole was and still is my favorite holiday song to sing, it's as if I can still close my eyes and hear the violins play the first few notes and I feel like a giddy little girl again. Every day I would wake up and beg my mother to open one gift before Christmas and every time I was met with a "no." But it did not deter me from trying until one day my mother finally gave into my cries and I heard a "yes." You must understand what a victory this was for me because when my mother said no, it was no and don't bother asking again. But this time I won! I dashed to the tree like a sprinter crossing the finish line and grabbed the first gift I could see. I ripped it open with such passion and I started screaming because in my hands I was holding a horse with wings from the cartoon from the 80's- *She-Ra*! If you are reading this right now and you were born during this era, then you know exactly what I am talking about. *She-Ra* was the Princess of Power; it was created as a spin off from another popular cartoon *He-Man*. But if you were born after this time I feel sorry for you because you missed out on one of the best cartoons ever. Thank God for YouTube because you can watch some of the episodes and become a She-Ra fan.

Even though my mother was stern in her ways, I know deep down in her heart it brought her great joy to see her daughter smiling from ear to ear, because she was giving me the life she never had. Now that I am a mother myself, it brings me great joy to see my daughter rip gifts open and run around the house like a maniac.

As I grew older, my mother always made sure she was planting the right seeds into my head. It was important to her that my brother and I made something of ourselves. Maybe it was because she at times felt like the underdog, whether it was due to her own up- bringing or some other reason, and she never wanted me to feel that way. This is when I learned one the most impactful lessons of my life- my voice mattered.

"One day I am not going to be around and you need to learn how to speak up for yourself, April. Don't ever let anyone take away your voice. At the end of the day everyone is human and not even the president of the United States could disrespect you. The only one you should ever fear is God."

Now I know this may sound a bit audacious, but she knew raising kids in the Bronx during the "crack era" would be tough. She was not only preparing my brother and me for the streets, she was preparing us for life. Over and over again my mother made sure I always knew who I was and how I should treat people.

She would tell me "Even if you see someone who is homeless or one of your friend's mothers is addicted to drugs, you treat them like a human being because you don't know their story."

I find those words to be so profound because everyone has a story to tell. You have a story. You have a voice that matters. It's so easy to go through this life comparing ourselves to others especially with so much access to the internet. We see celebrities taking amazing filtered selfies and wonder why we can never live up to those standards. Being a woman is hard enough and dealing with so much pressure to look a certain way can be overwhelming. So, no matter how hard it is for you at this moment, begin to love and accept yourself now. There is only one you in this world so make it count. I call that a "Maria-ism."

As much as my mother was adamant about me using my voice to empower others, I truly believe my mother never had anyone teach her she should dream big and live a life of purpose. Like I said, I don't know much about my mother's past and I am sure when she reads this she might disagree. But I can still remember the exact moment where I learned a poignant bit of information about why my mother had always been so tough and guarded. We were sitting in my parent's dining room table and casually talking about some issues going on in my family. And whenever there is an opportunity to learn more about my mom I do my best to listen because I know it's not easy for her to open up. We talked about how difficult it was for her and one of her sisters to be loving and affectionate to their children. As we continued the conversation I noticed my mother's mood shift and she became very quiet.

She was staring down at the table and asked me "Do you know when the first time I ever had a birthday cake was?"

I nodded my head no.

"When I was twenty-two years old."

My mother's lip was quivering and tears began to fall. "Your father was the one to celebrate me and I will never forget that."

I honestly didn't know how to react at first because it was so unexpected. I can count the moments where I have seen my mom open up the way she did and cry. So I just stood there with her and allowed her to be in the moment. I felt honored she would open up to me like that and allow me to see what was inside her heart. It was as if she needed to express those words for a long time and I was there to support her. For the first time I felt like I was able to hear her voice.

Have you ever felt as if your voice has never mattered? And I don't just mean your audible voice, I am referring to your voice as a whole. What do you believe in? What morals and standards do you live by? I like to refer to my voice as part of my soul. The thing that makes April who she is today as a woman. Have you been stripped of your voice and are trying to rediscover who you are? I know it might sometimes feel as if you will never find your voice but I want to encourage you to not give up on yourself.

My mother had no idea when she was raising me to be a strong proud Latina woman whose voice was powerful, that it would one day be silenced due to the violence. Because of the emotional abuse I endured I found I couldn't even recognize my own voice if I tried. So many times of hearing someone tell you "no one will ever love you again" can make you doubt yourself beyond measure. One of the saddest feelings in the world is to be in the presence of someone you love and they make you feel like the loneliest person in the world.

According to the U.S. Department of Justice women between the ages of 18-24 are most commonly abused by an intimate partner.

It would take me years to finally find my voice again.

I wish I could sit here and say I have had an amazing relationship with my mother all my life but I haven't. We have bumped heads many times before. She is one of the most complex women I know, has been emotional restricted with me since I can remember, but when my mother gave me access to see that little piece of her puzzle, I stopped blaming her.

Finally, I accepted my mother for who she is and let me tell you, it was an amazing feeling. She's not the fantasy mother I always dreamed of, but after listening to her I understood the nature of my mother, Maria Alvarado is and always has been a fighter. She has been fighting her entire life. And she wanted to make sure her daughter would be equipped to live in a world that can be very hard and cruel sometimes.

Just a few months ago I was having a conversation with a Pastor who knows me pretty well and he looked at me and said "April you are a fighter. You will have to fight some great battles because God has called you to great things."

For so long I resented the fact that I have had to fight for so many things in my life. I've had to fight my way out of depression, suicidal thoughts, and an abusive relationship just to name a few. But because I fought my way through all these things I am standing here today writing my first book. Praise God.

You might be in one of the biggest fights of your life right now. You may wonder why is it that I have to work so hard for everything while everyone else has it easy. Well first of all, stop comparing your life to everyone else. Secondly, it's all about perspective. Maybe you might want to ask God to help you see your situation in a different way. Maybe you have been asking the wrong question. Take a moment to really think about what it is you want to see happen in your life. This takes some practice but I guarantee if you learn how to be proactive and not so reactive you can really experience some major changes in your life.

`My mother has a very peculiar phrase and it goes like this, "Grab the bull by the b@lls."

As a child, I thought it was funny. As a teenager, I felt cool saying it. As an adult, she'd say it when I headed out to my auditions. One day I asked her where the saying came from, she told me she didn't quite know, but that it was to be utilized as a way to be ready to tackle anything that came my way in life. After many years of hearing this phrase I needed to develop for myself a subtext of what it meant for me to "Grab the bull by the b@lls," so here it goes.

A bull is a huge animal. The average bull can weigh in from 1600 to 1700 pounds. The purpose of a bullfighter is to conquer this massive bull. And if you have ever watched a bullfighter, they face the bull head on with such grace, confidence and determination. They know in the end they will be victorious and conquer the bull. When my mother said, "Grab the bull by the b@lls," she needed me to know I could conquer the world.

She was telling me in her own way, "You are a star. You don't need anyone to tell you. You have to know it."

I don't know what bull you are facing in your life today. Sometimes it doesn't have to be so traumatic and intense. It could be you figuring out what is your purpose in life. How do you use your voice in a way that could impact change? Everything you need to answer these questions is within you. And if you have left an abusive relationship and starting from scratch this is the best time to see your situation as a beginning and not an ending. There will be some fights in your life that may appear to be unfair but I truly believe it's in the fight where we discover has strong we really are. Your voice is one of the most powerful tools you have. It is time to start using it and speak life into your dreams and destiny. So, grab the bull by the b@lls and conquer the world!

Your Voice Is Powerful
Your Voice, Your Choice

- Can you describe a time when you felt your voice did not matter? How did it make you feel?

  _____

  _____

  _____

  _____

  _____

  _____

- Because words are so powerful please write down three positive words that best describes you!

  _____

  _____

  _____

- What are some of the ways you can use your voice to empower not only yourself but others around you?

  _____

  _____

  _____

  _____

  _____

  _____

  _____

  _____

  _____

Making Powerful Choices

I have traveled the United States meeting and speaking with thousands of students from all different age ranges. I have gone from middle school and high school to juvenile facilities and one of the common things I discovered while listening to many of their stories has been the absence of a father. I have witnessed kids emotionally break down in front of me because they desired so much to have a relationship with their dad, but did not have one and probably never would. My heart breaks every time and I am reminded of how blessed I have been to have experienced the love of my father. There are times when I watch my daughter play with my husband and a part of my heart fills with joy because I know she will never know what it's like to be a fatherless child. I am also very aware my story could have turned out completely different because there were choices my father made that probably could have ended his life. Felix Hernandez was born in the South Bronx-March, 1950.

"Back in my day all we did as kids was play stick ball, go to social clubs and watch the Yankees play."

Thurman Munson was my dad's all-time favorite Yankee, but his number one choice player was Roberto Clemente (who actually played for the Pittsburg Pirates). Clemente was also Puerto Rican and the first Latino to be inducted into the National Baseball Hall of Fame. Unfortunately, on December 31st, 1972, while en route to deliver aid to earthquake victims in Nicaragua, his plane crashed and Clemente passed away at the age of 38.

"My heart was broken when I found out Clemente died; he was a phenomenal player and a man of great integrity who just wanted to help people in need. They don't make players like that anymore; nowadays players are too full of themselves."

For over twenty years my father worked for the MTA (our transit service in NYC) as a cleaner. Every day he would have his daily routine where he would wake up at 4:15 in the morning and take a shower, read his newspaper, eat a balanced breakfast containing: cereal, orange juice and toast. By 5:15 he was out the house while my mother, brother and I slept. One of the things I will never forget was the smell of his cologne-

Grey Flannel, which permeated throughout the apartment and had a very manly scent. In a hound dog fashion, I would sniff for clues to see where my father had stepped in our home while we were sleeping. It made me feel so safe and appreciative how much my dad sacrificed for his family. So much so, that while removing his work boots one day I noticed a hole on the bottom of his sole. I am not sure if my father even remembers that particular moment, but it taught me so much about my father and about myself. At first I became angry. I was angry that my dad had to walk around with a hole in his shoe and I could do nothing about it. But on the other hand, it gave me this inner drive, and ignited a fire inside my soul to want to work harder than ever in my life to make my dreams come true. I made a choice in the moment to never ever allow my circumstances to dictate my future. You shouldn't either.

I truly felt like my dad was Superman. But even a super hero has a back story.

Dad enjoyed going to church and would get dressed on Sunday morning's in a polyester suit and head out the door to mass. Sometimes his sister would join him, but this Sunday she stayed home. When he returned from the service, he saw her there, brown eyes buried in a note, as she sat on the couch crying.

It was a note from their mother and it read like this: "Dear Felix, I can no longer be your mother."

At the tender age of 13, my father's world and all he knew would be forever changed when his mother abandoned him and his sister. A year later, my grandfather would leave to Puerto Rico and Felix Hernandez was left to fend for himself. If you ever come across my dad, he is the most loving, charismatic, and a loyal to a fault kind of man. Looking at him you would never know my dad was abandoned by his parents. You would never have guessed that in the future he would become the most amazing father in the world. He made a choice to love.

It wasn't until much later in my life that I learned this, but while growing up in the wild streets of the South Bronx, my father became addicted to heroin and struggled to survive.

"April, I was an evil man during those times and I felt like I was the devil and would hurt anyone. I was so full of rage and pain from being abandoned by my parents it drove me to do so many things I regret, but it also made me into the man I am today."

This was impossible for me to imagine because he had always been the kindest, gentlest and honorable man that I'd ever known. Now, on the opposite end of that, I'd seen what drugs like heroin did to people, and I wouldn't have wanted to witness that part of my father. I could see the weight of his shoulders just come right off when he was able to finally "confess" (in a way) his past to me, his daughter. I was so honored he would feel safe enough to reveal such a dark secret about his life because it was an unveiling moment for myself. I was not looking at my father, but I saw the human side of this man I love so much.

"April, in life there are going to be some choices you will have to make and it's up to you to choose how you will live your life no matter how bad or good it may be in the moment."

As you hold this book in your hand right now I want you to know no matter what has occurred in your past, no matter how bad you may think it could be, today is a new day to make the choice you need to live the life you have always desired.

At one point, he had succumbed so badly to his addiction that he went to his sister's home to rob her. He needed more money for drugs. But he was so high when he tried, he couldn't even complete the task of robbing her. His sister was married by that time, and my father forgot that her husband was at home. Her husband pulled a gun on him and gave him a choice. Well sort of.

"You find a program, you go to rehab, and you get clean, or you die. Which will it be?"

My father chose to live.

He experienced such a miraculous recovery while he was in rehabilitation that my father began to counsel other people who had the same issue as him. He discovered in helping others, he didn't need the drugs anymore and when it comes down to it- getting clean is a choice.

"You have to want to get clean more than you want to breathe it is the only way to really kick a drug habit."

"When I met your mother she was this fine woman with a huge afro and I knew I wanted to spend the rest of my life with her. I didn't have much but with my welfare check and odd jobs I was able to move us into an apartment. When mommy became pregnant and you and your brother were born, it was as if God had given me a second chance at life to redeem my past and I am grateful every day for the both of you."

Growing up with my father was a tremendous blessing. He was nurturing and kind and there was never a time, not once, I ever doubted his love for me. He always taught me I deserved to be respected and loved. He constantly made choices that would help others. I have never understood how he made the choice to continue to love and pay it forward in a world where he had been abandoned by the two people that were supposed to protect and love him unconditionally. No one ever showed him how to love but I truly believe God created him with a heart of Gold. I constantly remind my dad his greatest purpose in life was to be my father.

We don't have to continue to make bad choices. We can CHOOSE to change no matter what. He chose to allow himself to love someone. I have never seen a better example of a person who was dealt the worst hand of cards and came out a winner. Not because of good luck, but because of some kind of divine intervention and because he chose a path of love.

In the movie Freedom Writers, my character Eva didn't really have a choice when she was forced into a gang at a very young age. Her father went to jail and she was left to fend for herself as a little girl. Eva had to grow up really fast and protect not only herself, but her family legacy. At the beginning of the movie, you see Eva is extremely hesitant in trusting Erin Gruwell. She didn't trust anyone. In fact, not allowing anyone in was her was of protecting herself from harm. It wasn't until the end, in the courtroom scene where she had to make one of the most difficult decisions in her life, and that was to tell the truth and reveal Paco, her boyfriend murdered the young man in the store. Now if you have never watched the movie the Freedom Writers I highly suggest you do. Not just because I act in it, but because it is based on a true story about the real Freedom Writers, and it models so well the power of making a choice.

It is imperative you understand the choices you make in life not only affect you but it affects everyone around you as well. If my father would have allowed his situation of being abandoned by his parents to dictate the rest of his life, he could have easily done the same to us. Is it easy to make the right decision when someone has hurt you? No, it isn't. Is it easy to make excuses in life and ask yourself, what is the point of dreaming if no one even believes in me? Of course it is. But if you are holding this book, that means you are alive and breathing which tells me YOU have the power to change your life right now! Although I may never get to meet you in life, just know I believe in you because someone believed in me.

Some of the choices that you might need to make to get to the right place in your life will be difficult. It's your choice. Who do you need to forgive? What do you need to do to move on? It's a lot easier to place blame and complain than it is to be proactive and do something about your situation. Now go and make a powerful life changing choice!

Making Powerful Choices
Your Voice, Your Choice

- As we learned in this chapter making choices whether bad or good can really determine where we will end up in life. What choices do you believe you need to make today in order to move closer to your destiny?

  _____
  _____
  _____
  _____
  _____
  _____
  _____

- Once you have identified what the choices are, what is your plan of action to staying committed to them?

  _____
  _____
  _____
  _____
  _____
  _____
  _____

- Write down your new choices on a sheet of paper and hang them in a place where you will see them every day. Type them into your phone or you can create a hashtag and have other people join you!

LOVE IS PATIENT, Is Kind. It does not envy. It does not BOAST. IT IS NOT PROUD. It does not DISHONOR others, IT IS NOT {self-seeking} {easily angered} it keeps No Record of wrongs. LOVE — does not delight in evil — BUT REJOICES WITH THE TRUTH IT always trusts. always protects, always hopes, always perseveres.

1 CORINTHIANS 13:4-6

Love Is A Choice

1996 was a year of change for the people of New York City. We were hit with one of the biggest blizzards in eighteen years and it was so severe schools were closed down for days. The symbolic white snow (all thirty inches of it) blanketed most of the Bronx and everyone from my neighborhood took advantage of the no school policy. We all played together whether it was building snowmen, throwing snowballs from the rooftop, making angels in the snow or my favorite; tackle football- which by the way I excelled at. It was one of the best years of my life on Creston Avenue. Of course, things got back to normal quickly as soon as the snow melted and my sophomore year in high school came to an end. Faster than I could blink, summer approached and my life as I knew it then, would be forever changed.

I can still remember seeing him for the first time. He was beautiful, physically. I don't know if it was part of my soul or because of my immaturity, but I didn't for a moment imagine that anything ugly could be hiding behind his mesmerizing eyes. He was older. He was tattooed. He was a mother's nightmare and a teenager's wildest dream. I was naturally outgoing and a typical high school girl, unaware of my naivetés and convinced that I was invincible. How could I not have been? My father had never told me anything otherwise. My grades were good, I was on the honor roll, and I played softball and was the captain of that team and my volleyball team. My main purpose in life was to make people laugh. Being funny was at my core and I adored every aspect of being known as that girl. I was confident, proud, strong, and fearless as ever when I met him.

The connection was instant. Like a flip of a switch or the striking of a match, I was attracted to him immediately. He was in his early twenties, but he wasn't the first older boy that I'd been attracted to. I can't tell you why, but the boys my own age just didn't appeal to me.

"Grown men don't like to just hold hands." My mother would say while her eyebrow raised and her nostrils flared.

I would say to her "Aye mommy you don't know what you're talking about, he respects me and I understand him and he understands me". You know that teenage love, the one where we think we can never fall in love this deep again and whatever our parents said was always wrong. I was still a virgin, my heart was young and I was outrageously open-minded. My mother and I would fight constantly over him. I wonder if she had a sixth sense about him from the beginning sometimes, but she'd just complain that he was too old for me. But all of the boys I liked were too old for me. What made this boy any different?

The connection. The fact he wasn't a boy but a man or so I thought at the time. The first six months were everything I'd hoped it could be. We were in love. It was a wonderful and amazing first relationship. He was my first love. My first partner. My first sexual experience. I believed in waiting until I was married but it obviously did not happen and my mother was right he didn't want to just hold hands. So I gave the most sacred part of me to him and we were bonded together for the next three and a half years. All of it was everything that you could want it to be. We were Tony and Maria and even if the whole world was against us, we had each other.

"She isn't in love, she's merely insane." – West Side Story

Never once in those first six to nine months when we were dating did I ever think our love story would have had anything but a happy ending. We took care of one another. He grew up without a father and his mother was not the most nurturing, loving, attentive woman to her son. He needed me to be the loving, caring woman in his life, and I happily accepted the role.

I felt special when we'd go out together because he was an eclectic guy and while I was a few years younger than him, I had an old soul and was interested in many things you could say. I could hold a conversation and plus I was a dreamer. I would talk about so many of the things I wanted to accomplish when I became an adult and in my mind at the time I saw myself sharing these dreams with him and no one else. As previously mentioned I had no reason to believe he would ever intentionally hurt me because he loved me right? Well, not until the first time I saw and experienced the other side of him.

To this day I can't even tell you what we were arguing about. We weren't in a lonely room or a dark alleyway; we were standing right in front of my apartment door. My parents were inside and it was a regular day outside. The sun was shining. Children were playing and birds were chirping. Then it all went black.

The slap hit me with enough force to send saliva flying out of my mouth like a boxer who was about to get knocked out. I felt like I could see cheeks conforming to the pressure in slow motion as my head jerked back and forced me to come back to reality. I was silent.

I couldn't even react. I'm fairly certain I didn't even breathe. I couldn't move. I was frozen, not by fear, but by disbelief. It was like I knew for sure there was no way this moment was possibly happening in my world.

The shape of his eyes changed and he stared through me like a beast marking his territory. He didn't blink or sigh. He just ripped through me with his eyes. His solid five foot nine-inch frame towered over me, barely five feet tall, waiting for me to move, hoping I'd react so he could do it again.

"I hope you understand you just slapped me", were the only words I could murmur. There was still no reaction from him. I'm sure the whole incident was less than a minute long, but I felt like I'd been standing there for hours when my mouth finally moved.

"Leave!"

After several minutes passed he finally left. He did not whisper a sound. Inconspicuously, I opened the door and walked straight to the bathroom and locked myself in. My mind was racing and I was terrified of my parents finding out what just occurred outside the door. I washed my face with cold water trying to rid the imprint of his huge, calloused hand off of my face. I didn't cry. I didn't scream. I just looked at myself in the mirror and tried to understand what just happened between us. I couldn't. Every good memory, every kiss, was wiped away with one swift slap. I closed the door to my bedroom and slept for as long as I could.

Allow me to share something important. I didn't wake up the next day and resign myself to a life of abuse. I didn't say to myself, "I love him and if I have to live with a slap here and there, so be it." I woke up feeling sorry for him, telling myself he didn't mean to do it. If his mother hadn't been so terrible then he would never disrespect any woman especially me. I probably said something awful and I don't even remember doing it. He was my first love. I'd already given my virginity to him and I wasn't a quitter. We were in a real relationship and real relationships take work. I thought maybe if I love him a little more everything would be okay.

But everything wasn't okay. As a matter of fact, the day the slap took place was the day our entire relationship took a turn for the worst. The man I first fell in love with no longer existed. It didn't all happen at once, but day by day he'd take control of the little things in my life and eventually the abuse would occur more frequently. You see the purpose of an abuser is to have full power and control over the victim, utilizing tactics to keep them isolated from friends and family.

I stopped hanging out with my friends, one because I didn't want them to catch on to what was happening, and two because none of my friends or family really liked him anyway. Which was a huge sign for me but I could not see it at the moment. There was this one incident where he and I were supposed to go on a double date with my cousin. We had gotten into a heated argument and it was so bad I just called her and said we weren't going because he had no money. But it was a lie. I found myself lying more and more. Eventually I quit going to parties and every time I decided to go out, I'd cancel because he'd make me feel sorry for him because he didn't want to be alone. He couldn't be without me. I was necessary in his world. And as crazy as this may sound I loved him and could not abandon him the way everyone else did in his life. When he was not acting out I could see the gentleness inside of him, which kept me holding on but soon even that would change.

The abuse intensified and so did his tactics. One of his proudest moments was the time he purchased a brand new car on his own. We were excited to be able to go where ever we wanted but for me the car would soon become a place of terror. One evening while driving down the West Side highway, we of course, were arguing like always. He was driving like Mad Max on the road going about 95 miles and I was pleading with him to calm down. I can't even tell you verbatim what the fight was about but I remember him screaming at the top of his lungs "You want me to crash this car because I will and we will both die?" All I was trying to do in the moment was survive. When a person is experiencing any type of abuse the only thing they can do in the moment is do their best to survive another day. No one person in their right mind wakes up one day and says my dream in life is to be abused. No woman in her right frame of mind makes a decision to marry a man who will abuse and humiliate her.

But I still could not leave the relationship. Which is the one question people ask all the time is why does the victim stay? Well, if you yourself have never been abused in any way, whether it be sexually, physically, emotionally, financially, and or mentally, bless your heart for not ever having to experience such deep pain. But it is when you do find yourself in this type of situation where you wonder why did I stay? There are a thousand and one reasons why women stay. And my hope is that after you read this chapter you will get a clear answer why someone like myself would endure physical and emotional abuse for over three years.

I stayed because I was afraid.

I stayed because I was full of shame and embarrassment.

I stayed because I knew I would be judged if people found out the truth.

I stayed because I wanted to save him.

I stayed because I thought I loved him.

I stayed...

We fought about absolutely everything. He wanted me more than anything in the world, but there was nothing I could do to make him feel complete and I began to feel suffocated by him. That's when things started to get weird and scary, plus he was extremely jealous. Before dating him I had many guy friends because I was such a tomboy and I could hang with the guys. It just so happened that one of my closest guy friends and I were hanging out at the park playing softball. He kindly drove me home and when we pulled up to my building I started telling him how unhappy I was in my relationship. Simultaneously, my boyfriend happened to be walking towards my building to visit me. My heart stopped. Then it began to pound in my chest. In an instant I felt anxious and didn't know what to do. I begged my friend to quickly drive away but he suggested that I let him come out of the car and introduce himself. So I courageously stepped out and walked up to my boyfriend who was fuming with rage that I was with another guy. But I didn't have anything to hide. My friend introduced himself and was coldly greeted with a stern handshake. My friend got in his car and drove away. I wanted to go in the car with him to never return but I knew I was in for a long fight. We were standing in front of my building when he grabbed me by my shoulders and shoved me in, keep in mind, it was complete daylight. Anyone could have caught us fighting especially my dad. But no one did. While we were waiting for the elevator he was threatening me and calling me all kinds of derogatory names. He became so enraged he ripped the elevator door off the hinges. You would think I was in a wrestling match with the Hulk. These are just some of the things that went on in our relationship.

Inside, I was fully aware of the insanity. I wasn't in denial or pretending it was normal. I knew what was going on between us was wrong, but I wanted to fix him. I didn't want to give up. I couldn't abandon him even though it was wrong because he'd already been abandoned once.

Our fights got bigger and more violent. When we would begin, I would look into his eyes, trying to find the man I fell in love with, and I saw nothing. He was empty, blank and evil. That was when I did start to accept my fate. I knew our love story wasn't going to end well, but I was in it for the long haul. There were many times where I fought back but how much damage could I do to someone who was much taller and stronger than me. Sometimes in society it is assumed the victim doesn't even try to fight back but that is not always the case. Some of us fight, some of don't, either way it in no way means we are weak. All the time no one had an inkling of the abuse. I became an expert at hiding everything. People knew I was not happy in the relationship but they did not know to what extent. Abuse has a way of silencing your voice. *Silencing your dreams.* I hated who I had become.

By the time that I was a senior in high school, I felt like I was thirty years old. Everything in my world had changed. My good grades were a thing of the past and I just wanted to do whatever I could to get by. I started to lose my good girl reputation and gain a new one for being disrespectful to teachers. They were surely reaching out to me, trying to find the girl that they knew was inside, but I didn't care anymore. That girl was gone. She'd been beaten out of me. All that remained of her were the bloodstained clothes and the scars I tried to hide on a daily basis.

By the summer after graduation, I tried to find her again. I started to hang out with some friends and had been gone for the entire day, without my boyfriend. It was the first day in a long time I didn't feel anxious or scared. I was hanging out not too far from where he lived and it was almost one in the morning and we were all getting ready to head home. I found it a bit odd he and I did not communicate all day but didn't think much of it. I happened to look to my left and saw a guy walking towards me with two girls. It took me a minute to see it clearly, but when I did, I realized it was my boyfriend and he was holding hands with another girl.

My heart sank, but as usual, I didn't want anyone to notice. I tried not to react. My friends started freaking out asking me what I was going to do about it. For a second, I thought maybe he had moved on. Maybe I was finally free. I felt relief. A little piece of me started to spark back to life. That was before he made eye contact with me. I was in shock. I could not believe I caught him with another girl. When he saw me he let the girl's hand go and proceeded to walk towards me. I told my friends to leave.

I asked him "Who was that girl?" I started to lose my mind for the first time. I begged him for the truth. He then looked at me and said I looked like a whore because I had on a pair of shorts he didn't approve of. He accused me of wanting to get attention from guys and started to manipulate the situation and before I knew it, the entire fight was about me. I don't know why I went home with him, but I did. Before we even closed the door to his apartment, he grabbed my hair and flung me across the room. I looked towards the door and wondered if anyone had heard. Maybe someone was calling the police right then. I stood up and put my hands in front of my face.

He pushed me up against the wall next to the window and held me by the neck. I could hear the cars going by outside and see the lights of the city. Life was going on. People were rocking their babies and kissing one another good night, spooning next to their husbands and wives and praying for their families.

I was fighting for my life.

I felt this was going to be my last day on earth.

I didn't even realize he had lifted me up off of the ground by my neck until he threw me on to the couch. I started gasping, trying to catch my breath when he got on top of me. He tried to sexually force himself on me.

I was so scared and confused. I tried to push him off of me with everything I had.

"If you don't give it to me I'll go out and get it somewhere else, April."

I reached to the coffee table and grabbed the remote control, trying to smash it into his head. I broke free and ran across the room to the door. I knew I had to get away or I was going to die that night. I was going to be raped and killed and my story would be on the front of the newspapers the next morning. I opened the door and started screaming as loudly as I possibly could. He chased me down the stairs yanked me by the hair. I was hoping an old lady who had a screaming Chihuahua would run out her door and call the cops but it never happened.

"Now you are really going to get it." He whispered by my face as he grabbed my hair and dragged me up the stairs and back into his apartment. So many thoughts ran through my mind while I was doing my best to break free from his grip. It was as if my life flashed before my eyes and I could see my dad and hear his voice telling me the man who loves you will never put his hands on you. All the while I am being thrown around like a rag doll. I thought maybe if I leave my blood on the wall the police will have my DNA for evidence. Those were my thoughts. I was eighteen years old.

He beat me until 6am when everything finally stopped.

I didn't get to mention this in the beginning but I had worn a white t shirt with the shorts. By dawn, it was red.

He went over to the bathroom and returned with a first aid kit. He took out alcohol pads and proceeded to wipe my cuts and bruises. I could not believe what I was seeing.

I asked him to kill me. I begged him to end it all, to please just take my life. I was done. There was nothing left of me. I couldn't do it anymore and I didn't want to live.

He started to cry and tell me that none of this would have happened if he didn't love me so much. I didn't care. I didn't feel anything at that point, not even pity. I just wanted to go home and sleep. He begged me to stay but as soon as I knew I could leave, I did. I felt like one of the zombies from the show The Walking Dead.

I'm sure you are thinking that's the end of my story with domestic violence. But it wasn't. I didn't leave. I didn't know how to leave. My relationship with him was all I knew. There was no one to tell me how to get away. And the internet didn't even exist at that point so I felt completely helpless. Have you ever felt completely helpless in a situation? Has there been a time were you thought to yourself there is no way I am going to make it out alive? I am here to tell you there is help, there is hope, and you are more than just a victim. If you are or have been abused allow me to tell you it is not your end!

He may have beaten me but he didn't win. But I knew the relationship would eventually end up in turmoil if I did not find some way to escape especially because I myself began to show signs of aggression and rage. He was full of evil and I would scream at the top of my lungs that he brought the devil out of me. I felt absolutely crazy while we would fight and he would manipulate me so much I began to believe all the lies he said about me.

Once I entered college, I tried to push myself to play softball. It worked for a while and I made friends right away, but he was still there, waiting in the shadows. I got to a point where I thought if I just ignored him, maybe he would go away. I thought if I wasn't giving him what he needed, he would go somewhere else and maybe want to stay there. He started to stalk me; told me that he couldn't let me go and there was no way he could ever stop loving me. I didn't care anymore, I wasn't afraid of him and I wasn't afraid to die. All of it became normal. The beatings were normal, life with him hiding and watching was normal. I accepted this was my life and I was simply waiting to die. I didn't believe in the possibility of a future and every time I started to, he crushed those dreams with his fists.

A year later, I was tired of waiting for him to kill me and decided I was going to do it myself. I was either going to slit my wrists or take some pills. There was no other way to stop the demon. I was alone in my room and by that time it was so hard to get out of bed because of the deep depression I was in. I had no will to live any longer. I was broken inside and out. The young, tough, vibrant Puerto Rican girl from Creston Avenue existed no more. All the while I am in my room contemplating my death, my parents who I loved so much, were outside not even aware of the severity. Not because they didn't care but because I never wanted them to know my secret. I had let them down so much I felt like I could never redeem myself in their eyes. I wanted so badly to run into my father's arms and have him tell me everything would be ok but I didn't. Abuse has the tendency to make you believe you don't deserve to be loved and live a life of success and purpose. Abuse kills dreams. It almost killed mine.

My room was the only place I felt safe. It was also where I let out most of my aggression. I would punch the walls, rip things apart, and scream into my pillow because I needed to find some way of releasing of the negative energy. I punched a mirror and it shattered to a point where when I looked in the mirror my face was distorted. I stared at myself for a few minutes and I could not recognize myself at all in that moment.

I cried.

I began to sob.
I came to my knees and I lifted my hands in the air and in the midst of sobbing I pleaded with God and I said "God if you are real please save me. Because if you don't I will die and I am not ready to leave this earth." I can't tell you anything profound happened in the moment, but something shifted.

God had a plan for my life. He has a plan for you as well.

It didn't happen immediately, but one day I woke up and I made one of the most difficult and best choices in my life- I decided to end my relationship with him. I called him over to my house and in my bedroom I said I was ending our relationship. He didn't take it very well, which was expected. And for the next six hours he was begging me to stay with him and telling me he was going to change and he was so sorry for what he had done. But I had made up my mind and I was not giving in to his lies.

As expected, he began to act out violently but to the point where no one could really hear him. He was choking me and again trying to force himself on me. He saw I was finally done this time. There was no going back. I made my choice to live again. I was done with the beatings, the name calling, the manipulations, and most certainly done with him as a whole. Finally, he left in a fit of rage, spit on my mirror and destroyed the mailboxes and intercom in our apartment building. Somehow, God kept my family from being held responsible for all of the damage he caused.

1 in 4 women will experience domestic violence. I was one out of the four.

Never in my wildest dreams did I ever think I would be the girl to end up in an abusive relationship, especially because I did not grow up in an abusive home. Which is the stigma that accompanies abuse; we are expected to come from a broken home or be abused as a child. But I am here to tell you abuse can happen to anyone, at anytime, anywhere in the world. Abuse is neither prejudice nor racist.

I am a survivor of Teen Dating Violence.

According to the Department of Justice, girls and young women between the ages of 16 and 24 experience the highest rate of intimate partner violence — almost triple the national average.

If you or someone you know has been abused, please do not be afraid to speak up.

Love Is A Choice
Your Voice, Your Choice

- These are some warning signs you may be in an abusive relationship:

  - If you are with a partner who...
    - is extremely jealous.
    - is controlling.
    - isolates you from family and friends.
    - checks on your social media without your permission.
    - is belittling and call you names.
    - makes you feel less than of a person.
    - instills fear not love.
    - has an explosive temper.
    - stalks you.
    - bullies you.
    - makes you feel there is no way out of this relationship.
    - threatens to commit suicide if you leave them.
    - pressures you to commit sexual acts against your will.

- Here are some common characteristics of an abuser. Keep in mind every abuser may be different but studies have shown most of them may use some of the same tactics.

  - An abuser at first may be pleasant and loving in the beginning of the relationship.
  - An abuser may suffer from low self-esteem and uses the violence to control.
  - An abuser may often deny any motive for violent behavior making the victim feel as though they are responsible.

- o An abuser often will try to ask for forgiveness and promise it will never happen again.
- o An abuser may go through periods where they are not as abusive as other times.
- o An abuser often objectifies the victim seeing them as their property or sexual objects.
- o An abuser doesn't have to necessarily come from a broken home or a broken situation. Some make a choice to abuse.

- If you are or have been in an abusive relationship, please go to the resource page of this book to receive the help you need.

- Abuse is abuse no matter what. Abuse is not love. If you at any moment feel you are in an abusive relationship or you know someone who is in one right now, please speak up. I know how scared you may feel to say something but you never know speaking up or reaching out can change your life. As I said earlier, there are resources at the end of this book please use them. Your life matters.

Intimate Partner Violence

Let's take a break from my story for a moment and talk about what you need to be looking for when it comes to really understanding Intimate Partner Violence. Do you think there is a chance you have been a victim of Intimate Partner Violence or do you think you might know someone who has? The basic definition of Domestic Violence also known as Intimate Partner Violence is, "a pattern of abusive behavior that keeps one partner in a position of power over the other through the use of fear, intimidation and control. It may manifest itself as physical, sexual, verbal, emotional, spiritual and financial abuse.

Gender violence, interpersonal violence, child abuse, teen relationship violence and elder abuse are all examples of domestic violence. Domestic violence is pervasive and occurs in all groups, regardless of race/ethnicity, income, age, education, religion, immigration status, or sexual orientation. It is rooted in sexism, racism and a culture of permissive violence."

According to the CDC, 33% of high school students reported having experienced both sexual and physical abuse. Of those, 25% of women and girls were between the ages of 11 and 17 and experienced the violence from someone that they considered a boyfriend or partner. If we turn those percentages into numbers, they mean that 1.5 million teenagers have been in an abusive relationship at some time in their lives between the ages of 11 and 17. That's one in every three teenagers. The statistics get even worse if you add just seven years to that demographic. 43% of college students, particularly females, report being victim to sexual, physical or emotional abuse. In addition, those students have told their partner everything about themselves and shared things like social media passwords, banking information, and email and financial information that can be used to threaten them after the abuse. 16% of those abused were subjected to internet stalking after ending the relationship.

Fifty percent of teens who are involved in an abusive relationship will try to commit suicide.

Why is that? Because only 1/3 of those who are victims of domestic violence talk about it to someone. which means that 75% of the victims keep it all bottled up and think they can't confide in anyone what they are going through. That's what happened to me. And I did think about suicide. It's even harder for some people who are going through this because in eight states, being abused while you are in a relationship or dating someone is not even considered a crime. So if the victim wants to get out, they cannot apply for a restraining order, they have to get out on their own. If you are reading this and you've felt there is no way out, please even if it's just one time, talk to someone. There are people out there who will listen to you and are not going to judge you or blame you. The resource page I have created in the back of this book is full of websites and numbers you can call and talk to people who are trained to assist you in any way. You are more than the violence; you are a person who deserves to be in a loving and healthy relationship.

Maybe you aren't sure if you are in a relationship that involves domestic violence or intimate partner violence. Ask yourself these questions:

- Are you afraid of your partner?

- Does your partner make you feel stupid or shout at you?

- Have you stopped talking about things that you know might make your partner angry?

- Do you feel like everything you do is wrong?

- Are you embarrassed to talk to your friends and family about your relationship?

- Do you blame yourself and believe you deserve the things your partner says and does?

- Is your partner jealous about everything?

- Does your partner hurt you, or *threaten* to hurt or kill you or someone that you love?

- Does your partner tell you where you can or cannot go?

- Can you see your friends and family when you want to, or does your partner control when you see them?

- Does your partner threaten to commit suicide if you leave?

- Are you limited when it comes to your access to money or transportation away from your partner?

- Does your partner force you to have sex?

Even if you feel like your partner only does a few of these things, or maybe only does them sometimes, even the most minor hint of domestic violence has the ability to turn into a major situation. Are you telling yourself things are only emotional and verbal right now, and that you aren't being hurt physically? Well, emotional and verbal abuse is just as big of a deal as the physical.

A person who is abusing you emotionally or verbally is trying to slowly take away the things that make you feel worthy and able to do things on your own. They may also make you feel worthless and without them there is no way out of the relationship. These are tactics that are referred to as power and control.   According to the Domestic Abuse Intervention Project (DAIP) they developed the Power and Control wheel as a visual aid to describe the most common abusive behaviors or tactics used against women. Now the reason I refer to women is because women are killed 3.5 times more often than men in domestic homicides.

Whether you are going through physical or emotional and verbal abuse, you need to remember it happens in a cycles. So, just because your partner is acting normal today, doesn't mean they've changed their ways.

Many times when I hear survivors speak about their abuse whether it is from heterosexual relationships or from the LGBTQ community, I usually hear them say something like "He was an amazing man and swept me off my feet, but then out of nowhere one day he slapped me across the face." The first time my abuser slapped me was definitely the beginning stages of the abuse. And it would continue in cycles so there were times where he was very sweet and loving to me, and then it would shift to him just being extremely abusive, especially emotionally.

Most times after the abuse happens, your partner will apologize and tell you how sorry they are for their actions and promise it will never happen again. This is the guilt stage of the cycle. Once your partner is through with feeling guilty, they will then start to come up with all sorts of excuses why they did what they did to you. They may blame themselves or may blame you, but overall, they are excuses. After you've gotten through the excuses and the blame game, that's when you might start to believe it was a "one-time thing" and your partner just had a hiccup. They will act normal and behave like you are in a regular relationship. This may confuse the victim and make them believe it will never happen again.

So, how do you get out? Have you ever felt like there is no way that you will get out alive, like I felt? This is probably the most difficult thing to write, but studies have shown it takes a woman about 7 to 8 times of being abused before she finally gets to leave the relationship. Now keep in mind this is also based on the duration of the relationship. There are some who will be in an abusive relationship from 6 months to over 20 years. I really wish I could tell you that after reading my book all of your problems will be solved and you will be able to leave right away if you just speak up, but doesn't always work out that easily. What I am providing is hope, an outlet and resources for you so you don't feel alone. When I was going through my situation there were no outlets I was aware of, especially for a teenage girl. I never really felt safe sharing my story with anyone because I was just simply ashamed and didn't think I could get the help I needed. But that does not have to be your story.

Finding someone to talk to is the most important part of the process in leaving an abusive relationship. If you feel like you can't talk to your parents or someone else in your family, you can start by finding a place where you know you will be safe; it can be a place of worship, a medical doctor, or a school counselor.

You can also look for a domestic violence program in your city and become educated about your situation. In some cases, not all it is best if you can keep a journal and write down how you are feeling and what is happening to you as evidence. If things escalate and police have to get involved having tangible records like text messages, voice messages, or a journal can make your case much more powerful.

What if you aren't the one in an abusive relationship, but you think that you might know someone who is? There are lots of signs that can point to a person being involved with domestic violence.

- They may always seem like they are trying incredibly hard to make their partner happy.

- Even when it's not typically something they would do, they go along with their partner to make them happy.

- When you are with your friend, they may constantly check in with their partner.

- On the opposite end, the partner may constantly be texting, calling or harassing your friend.

- Your friend may try to passively bring up their partner's temper or jealousy without outwardly saying anything specific.

- Maybe your friend used to be really confident, but suddenly they seem to have very low self-esteem.

- Or, your friend used to be really friendly, but now they are withdrawn.

- They may act anxious all of the time or even talk about suicide openly.

- Your friend isn't allowed to hang out whenever they want to, and they have to ask permission from their partner before telling you yes or no.

- Lots of "accidents" have been happening to your friend causing physical injuries. Suddenly they've been "tripping" a lot.

- All of the sudden, your friend is missing school or work or other events that they would have normally attended.

- Their grades have declined.

So what do you do if you have a friend you believe is in an abusive relationship? You have to remain calm and just do your best to listen. No matter what, don't ignore the signs of abuse you think that you might be noticing. Tell your friend some of the specific things that you've noticed and have you worried about them. Make sure that your friend knows that you aren't going to judge them or tell them that the situation is their fault. It's pretty likely they already blame themselves and feel incredibly insecure about their situation. Tell your friend you are worried about them. Try to make all of the great things about them very clear. Point out all of the strengths and positive aspects about them over and over again. Remind them all of the gifts they have that makes them awesome. It may not guarantee them leaving the relationship right away, but they know they can feel safe around you which is so crucial in helping someone in this kind of situation.

One thing you must remember as the friend of a victim, you should never get into a position where you are in a risky situation with your friend's partner. You should never try to get in the middle or solve their problems. If you are there when your friend is hurt, you should call 911.

If you are reading this and you think maybe you are the one who has been an abuser in a relationship, you need to know that you can change. Your life doesn't have to be this way. You can break the cycle of abuse that you feel is turning your world in circles. You must remember that making any kind of change isn't easy and it's not going to happen overnight. Just like the victim, the abuser cannot change alone. You need help. Most likely, you are leaning on certain things to justify what you have done. But if you find help, whether it is through a pastor or church, a doctor or counselor, or by reaching out to one of the resources listed in the back of this book, you can change and you can learn how fulfilling a healthy, loving relationship can actually be. Please remember though, no matter how hard you try, you cannot do this alone. It will be scary admitting you have a problem, but imagine how scary your world will become if you don't change. There are people out there that will not judge you or condemn you, people who love you with the same love that God has for you and want to see you just as happy in life as your victim. It's going to take a lot of commitment and it won't be easy. But you were made to be so much more than an abuser. God's plan for you forgives the violence and will lead you down a path of happiness that you might not have known existed.

There are so many terrible and obvious things that happen to people who are in abusive relationships. The obvious ones, like getting hurt or killed, are ones that everyone knows about and can understand. But there are many more things that happen to the victims of domestic violence that often go unnoticed.

Teenage girls who have been abused physically or sexually are six times more likely to get pregnant or catch a sexually transmitted disease. In addition, girls who have been in an abusive relationship are eighty percent more likely to have a stroke and have a seventy percent increased change of developing heart disease. Most likely, girls who've been a victim of domestic violence are more likely to fall victim to long-term chronic health conditions like obesity and arthritis. Teens will have lower grades and a higher chance of abusing alcohol and drugs versus a teen who has not been a victim.

You must remember that intimate partner violence is not contagious. You won't catch it by helping a friend and you won't spread it by reaching out to someone. In fact, the more you try to keep it hidden, the more dangerous it becomes. Your voice matters and you can make a choice to break the cycle today. All it takes is the one step at a time. You are not alone.

Intimate Partner Violence
Your Voice, Your Choice

- Here is a list of the different types of abuse:
    - Physical abuse.
    - Emotional, Psychological, and Mental abuse.
    - Verbal abuse.
    - Financial abuse.
    - Spiritual abuse.
    - Sexual abuse.
    - Cyber bullying.

The Duluth Model or Domestic Abuse Intervention Project is a program developed to reduce domestic violence against women. It is named after Duluth, Minnesota, the city where it was developed.[1] The program was largely founded by Ellen Pence and Michael Paymar.[1]

Know Your Worth

The pop star, Rihanna, released a song a few years ago called *"We Found love."* One of the verses says "we found love in a hopeless place, we found love in a hopeless place." Every time I hear that song it makes me reflect on my relationship with my husband Jose. We began dating when I was 21 years old and he was 24 at the time, and the both of us were damaged goods. Jose was recovering from a relationship which left him depleted and heart broken, actually, he vowed he was not going to allow himself to get serious with anyone. And for myself, I was single and ready to conquer the world and go after my dreams. After leaving my abusive relationship I was determined to never allow anyone to get in my way of becoming successful. I was on a mission to become famous! I had no idea how I would get there but I believed in myself so much. All I had were my dreams.

For so long I felt worthless and didn't think I deserved anything in life especially when it came to love. I vowed to close my heart and never allow another man to hurt me the way my ex- boyfriend did. I know so many women who struggle with not understanding their own worth. I mean who can, when all they have experienced is abuse, lies, deception, and deep pain. So many of us who actually survive an abusive relationship don't even bother seeking therapy because it is frightening to have to sit and recall everything that happened in the past. We are also afraid of being re-victimized by someone or the justice system that doesn't understand why a woman would remain in an abusive relationship. Sometimes it's just easier to remain silent.

Surviving wasn't enough for me. I was not going to ever allow my voice to be silenced again.

So, Jose and I began dating and we fell for each other so fast it was absolutely terrifying and exciting at the same time. It was terrifying; because neither of us was looking for love. It was exciting; because we found love in a hopeless place. For the first time in a very long time I actually felt safe to be in the presence of a man. We felt like it could be love and were willing to risk many things to give the relationship a chance. In the beginning everything was amazing and wonderful. And they were, don't get me wrong, but I didn't realize at the moment I still had so much baggage from the past. Honestly I thought I was doing great, but an argument between us would reveal so much more about me.

Jose was still living with his parents. We were in his room having a heated discussion and all I remember was that Jose said something I apparently didn't like. I responded to him in a very demeaning way. He looked at me for a while, and in a very tender moment he grabbed my hand, stared at me straight in the eyes and said "I love you April but you can never speak to me like that again. I know you were hurt in your last relationship but I'm not that guy. I love you, but I love me more, and I cannot tolerate being disrespected by you or any woman."

I stood there in complete silence while my brain and heart were trying to process what just occurred. Then I began to cry in his arms because I was sorry I that spoke to him the way I did. That moment also exposed the reality that I was still damaged.

But it would not be the last time my anger would get the best of me.

Another time we were arguing and Jose (who happens to be about 5'10), got close up to my face and I completely lost my mind. I went blank and was ready to fight this man standing in front of me. I felt like a raging mad woman pounding my chest like King Kong screaming at the top of my lungs "Come on let's go you want to fight? I am ready!"

Jose just stood there once again staring at me and probably thinking to himself "this woman is definitely insane." I wasn't insane, but I most certainly had unresolved issues and at any moment the beast sleeping inside me could wake up and take over my life.

What most people who are victims of Intimate Partner Violence don't realize is that the healing period is very, very long. You don't recover overnight and even when you feel like you are past it, you probably aren't. Then there are the "unseen" consequences of abuse which may last a long time. There are so many emotional struggles remaining long after the abuse has ended. Depression, anxiety, insecurity, and falling back in to old habits are very common. All of these symptoms are a part of post-traumatic stress disorder (PTSD). Recent studies show that the majority of those who have been subjected to domestic violence and abuse suffer from PTSD and don't even realize it. Some of the symptoms are recurring nightmares or unwanted memories about the abuse, physical sicknesses like headaches and ulcers, feeling jumpy, anxious or angry all the time with a predisposition to become violent or irrational very easily.

So there I was, pushing my way right back into the violent kind of relationship I was finally free of. Jose is this gentle, quiet, man with kind eyes that looked through my pain and into my soul. The meaner I got, the kinder his eyes were. He wasn't looking at me with pity, but he was simply waiting for me to realize what I was doing.

For the first time in a long time, I realized what communication in a real relationship was like. I recognized what was very likely PTSD in me and knew that I was going to struggle with my rage for a long time, but it was something I could conquer. I was so angry inside and I wondered if the damage could ever be repaired. However, I realized in that moment if anyone could help me in my journey was Jose. For the first time, someone put me in check and I realized that just because I went through something terrible didn't mean I had the power or right to project my pain on someone else. Jose did not have to accept me treating him in an aggressive manner.

When you are in an abusive relationship and you see signs that things are going downhill and you don't do anything about it, it begins to fester. Moment by moment you accept it and plant the seed that can grow into one of two things: a beautiful relationship or a monster. You are making a choice in every moment, with every word. A violent relationship has to be fed to survive, just as a loving one needs to be fed in order to bloom. It blew me away when Jose told me he loved himself enough and was willing to let me go because- he knew his worth. I came to the realization I did not recognize my own worth. Yes, I was trying to move on from everything and was so focused on becoming this star, but deep down inside I really had forgotten how wonderful and amazing I was. And I say that in the most modest way, because I know it can sound a bit vain, but I needed to love me again. Even as I write, I wonder what would have happened if I had told my boyfriend after the first time he slapped me "I love you but I love me more and it's over." I know we are not supposed to dwell in the past but once in a while I really think about how my life would have been completely different if I would have left after the first time. I know for sure I would not be writing my story and sharing it with the world. I always tell Jose his love saved me from myself. His tolerance and patience showed me I was more than my rage and anger. I was worth so much more.

If Jose hadn't taken the time to put me in my place, I'm sure our relationship would not have lasted. At that point there was a shift inside of me. I suddenly knew Jose did not deserve to be treated that way, just like I didn't deserve it. It wasn't my fault.

Hurt people; *hurt* people.

When you are operating from a place of hurt, you realize you hurt others in order to try and make them understand what you are feeling. You don't necessarily want to hurt them but you also want to prove you have the power. Knowing your worth means you don't have to prove it. When you forget your worth, when you are suffering from the aftermath of the abuse, you cut yourself off from everything. You lose forgiveness, you become damaged and that damage is your only comfort. Loneliness takes you over.

Years after that day and long after I fully realized my worth, I knew in my heart I wanted to help others realize theirs. I especially wanted to work with teenagers and women because I knew I had something to give. In my career, as a speaker, taking courses and growing in the areas of understanding the dynamics of Intimate Partner Violence was essential. I was given an amazing opportunity to study under Dr. Rev. Alfred Correa and became certified as a Youth Chaplain. This meant I completed a program that equipped me with the tools to work with incarcerated youth. For about two years my husband and I visited juvenile facilities throughout the five boroughs working with this specific group of youth. In the two years of sitting and listening to these young ladies speak, the hardest thing to hear was how some of them felt there was no hope for them when they eventually left the facility. They were certain there was no way out.

As I sat in one of the sessions, listening to their stories instead of teaching one day, the pain in their voices was tangible. One girl opened up to the group and said that she was so afraid when she got out of the juvenile facility she wouldn't have anything to go home to. Her words reminded me of myself so greatly as she was sure no one cared about her, so there was really no point in her caring for herself. She was alone and she knew it. She'd messed up beyond forgiveness. There were so many things I wanted to tell her right then, but I chose to wait. It was time for me to listen. She needed to recognize I was listening to her voice. Her voice was being heard and that was enough. Finally, someone listened. No orders, no "this is how to fix you," just two eyes that could see her pain and two ears that were not going anywhere until she was done talking.

Another girl openly revealed she was a prostitute, and the only power she had was when she sold her body because she could control which John she slept with. My heart sank when I heard her story because despite what was happening, that was her reality. She had a child to raise and pimp to pay and that was all she knew. Her worth came from sleeping with men for money. This is all she knew how to do to survive.

She was fourteen.

I began to tell her I had no idea what it must be like to be in that kind of situation. I wasn't going to try to fake any emotion to make her feel better. I just listened. I wanted her to know at the moment her voice was being heard and her story mattered. I knew in about an hour I would have to leave these young ladies and they would return to their reality. But I did let her and the other girls know one thing and it was this; their reality was not their destiny. Despite where they were in life at the moment, which was a juvenile facility, this place was not their ending but it could be their beginning.

As tears streamed down my face I told her, "you are worthy, you are more. You might not be able to feel it right now and you might not even care, but you are more. You can feel again."

Everyone has experienced pain, everyone has hurt, and though it may be different types of hurt, in the end we all have the power to change. We have the power. You have the power. Those girls didn't know that they were worth more. It will take so much time that it will feel like it's never going to happen, but it will. You WILL want to give up, but I refuse to let you.

YOU ARE MORE.

After that day, I promised God I would continue to speak to anyone who needed to hear how worthy they were. It's hard to tell people that a God exists within such turmoil and pain. It's even harder for them to believe it when life and our situations are saying something completely different. There comes a moment where you can see they are starting to believe in themselves and it is beautiful. Standing on the outside and witnessing them start to believe in their voices again, watching the flicker of light echo from their souls, was enough to keep me pushing forward in healing myself, with the hopes that my voice, the one that I had finally found, could impact the world.

I want to remind you of this: *You will want to quit. You will try to find ways that are not always the best to make you feel worthy. You will cry. You will doubt. But keep pushing forward. You are worth it!*

It took many years and countless amounts of therapy sessions for me to get to a place where I understood the value of my worth. Especially in my line of work in the entertainment business, people are constantly judging me whether it's on my appearance or how relevant I am, and it can take a toll on my self-confidence. So I have had to work on me, inside and out, and realize the only one who can dictate how much I am worth is God and myself. The moment I allow the outside world to influence my thoughts it can send me down a very dark hole. So I whip my hair to the side, raise my eyebrow and say "I am wonderfully and fearfully made!" You should try that sometime and let me know how it goes.

Rhonda Rousey is probably one of the most notable athletes in the world at this very moment as I am writing my book. She is an undefeated MMA fighter (Mixed Martial Arts) and in her recent fight, she beat her opponent in 34 seconds. She is my hero. I have never seen a woman exude such confidence without having to use her sex appeal, which is a breath of fresh air. But the reason I mention her is because she absolutely knows her worth. That is the prime example of what I am trying to convey in this chapter. Rousey said in an interview "Some people like to call me cocky or arrogant, but I just think 'how dare you assume I should think any less of myself.' The problem isn't me thinking I can achieve any goal I set for myself, the problem is you projecting your own self-doubt onto me." Can I get an Amen to that?! Lesson learned: *don't allow anyone to determine your worth!*

Now as a mother I have the opportunity to teach my daughter, Summer Rose, how worthy she is. How much her voice matters even at the early age of three. She is learning from her father and me, and not from what the world tells her. My mother made sure she embedded my worth into my head, and taught me that I must love and honor myself no matter what.

You must do the same.

If there is anything that I can share with you today, it is how worthy you are. You are worthy of love and laughter and happiness no matter where you come from, what you've done, or what anyone has ever told you. You are not invisible, people can see you, the world can hear your voice, and most importantly so does God. He hears the cries of your voice, even in the moments where the world is screaming so loudly. Your cries are worthy of being heard and He is listening.

You might not know it yet, but you have something to share with the world. There is a reason you were put on this earth. Just like the makeup L'Oreal commercial says "Because, you're worth it!"

Know Your Worth
Your Voice, Your Choice

- What are some ways you can begin working on believing in your worth?

  _____

  _____

  _____

  _____

  _____

  _____

- When was there a time where you felt worthless?

  _____

  _____

  _____

  _____

  _____

  _____

- What are some of the things you love most about yourself?

  _____

  _____

  _____

  _____

  _____

  _____

Make Your Mess Into A Message

I don't remember a light going off inside of me whispering, "If you share it, they will come." There wasn't a specific event where I suddenly realized I wanted to tell the world all of my deep, dark secrets. But in 2010, I finally built up the courage to share my story of being a survivor of Intimate Partner Violence. I guess I was ready to finally talk about it for a couple of reasons. First, a few years had already passed where I felt strong enough to be able to share my experience from a place of power and not pain. God had done so much work on my heart, especially after getting married where I didn't feel like a victim anymore. I had survived and was seeking to really grow in so many areas of my life. Secondly, I realized I had a platform because of my status of being an actor and I remember one day as I was praying God asking me "what was I going to do about my past experiences.

Was I going to just keep it to myself or was I going to share my story with someone who had been in the same situation as me?" I felt so convicted in my spirit and I knew I had to do something.
So I did.

There are millions of women, children, and men who are being abused right this very moment. 1 in 4 women will experience domestic violence in her lifetime. This statistic is too much for me to fathom.

But before I could share my story with the world, I knew I had the responsibility to sit down with the two people who raised me to be strong. The two people who gave me my voice, who taught me about making powerful choices and to love myself; my parents. Up until that day, to my knowledge, they had absolutely no idea their daughter was carrying this secret around for so many years. I am sure they might have had an inkling but not to the full extent of my relationship with my ex. It was a secret that was holding me back from my freedom and when I let it go, when I finally opened up, I felt like a new person, I finally felt like I had let go of it all.

I am sure I am not alone on this, but have you ever felt like you were in such a "deep mess or a severe storm" where you probably thought to yourself, "Will I ever get out of this situation? Will I ever love again? Will someone truly love me if they knew my deepest secret? Will I ever reach a point where I love myself? Can I trust again?"

These are all valid questions to ask. Now I am not a therapist by a long shot, but what I can offer is a "*yes.*" *Yes,* you will love again; *yes,* you will trust again as long as you are willing to do the work on yourself. Because no matter how bad a situation may seem at the end of the day, it is up to you, the individual, to make a choice on whether you stay in or out the mess! My Pastor once told me something that was so profound I have never forgotten his words. I was in a messy situation and was seeking some guidance and he looked at me and said "April, in this life some people get it and some people don't. You need to decide which person you want to be and once you make that decision stick with it no matter what." That was a few years ago and I still use his advice often.

So I ask you "Some people get it and some people don't; which person do you choose to be in this life?"

Once you reach the transformational point that you finally let go of all your pain, fears, anxieties, and disappointments and allow love to take over, you will begin to experience life in a way you have never imagined. But before this can ever occur, it is imperative you identify those things in your life that have hindered you from fully becoming the person you were created to be. Listen, no matter what race, religious background, or sexual orientation you come from, the one thing we all have in common is our emotions. If you have experienced abuse in any way (and even if you haven't), you know first-hand that our emotions can lead us to make many irrational decisions. Because I felt emotionally strong to finally share my "mess," I knew I had to start by telling the truth to my father.

We sat on the steps in front of the building, just the two of us as we had done so many times in the past. Right then, I felt like a five-year old little girl with big brown eyes looking up at my daddy, preparing to divulge all of my secrets to him. I was petrified. I didn't know if he would judge me. I was afraid that my words would hurt him and he wouldn't look at me the same. So, I took a deep, deep breath and said, "Daddy I have something to tell you. I...um...I was in an abusive relationship with my ex. I have been holding this in for over ten years. I am so, so sorry." I began sobbing when I finally told him.

He was silent.

My emotions overwhelmed my words and the crying wasn't from the pain but finally feeling free from the past.

I reassured him that it wasn't his fault.

He was very quiet and finally asked, "why didn't you tell me, why didn't you let me help?" I tried to lighten the heaviness of the moment. I told him he's a crazy old school Puerto Rican who would have tried to retaliate. I didn't want him to go to jail. Then I really would have had no one to protect me. Now just so I am clear, this was how I handled my own personal experience. I would never, and I repeat never, advise anyone to do what I did- and that was to keep the abuse to myself. I know how hard it is to speak up to anyone, but we must not remain silent.

Abuse is NEVER acceptable in any way, form, or fashion.

He was angry. His anger wasn't with me, but with the situation and the fact that I had even been exposed to the violence. He was also angry that I went through it all alone. His baby girl had been hurt by someone and he could not save me at the time. I must have done an excellent job of hiding it, because he was very shocked. It was an extremely powerful moment for the both of us. After the tears, hugs, and questions we both felt this intense bond with one another. There were no more lies between us. A father and daughter were exposed to one another in the most vulnerable and honest way. And suddenly everything was ok. Everything was always going to be ok moving forward. We had each other and we respected each other. He didn't judge me and told me that he was proud of me. He was proud that I realized what was happening and I got out of the situation. He was even more proud I was going to tell my story to the public.

Why do I write about this moment to you, the reader? Because I need you to know and understand there is a story inside of you right now. If you found the courage to share it, you have no idea the impact you could have in someone's life. I have come to understand healing happens in community. For instance, have you ever told your story to a complete stranger and after leaving them you felt so much better after the fact? Or when you hear someone on television like a celebrity talk about something very personal, do you connect with them on a human level? Well, that's because when we realize we are not the only ones who experience pain, it makes us feel so much better. Stories of hardship and triumph give us hope in our own lives. This book is a testament on how

I decided to take my mess of abuse and create a message of love, hope and inspiration.

You can do the same.

Anne Frank is another example of someone who was in a very messy and scary situation and decided to record her life in a journal. If you have never read the Diary of Anne Frank, I really implore you should. At the age of 13 Anne was given a journal on her birthday by her father. Unfortunately, within a few months their lives would be forever changed. They would have to go into hiding and live in an attic for the next two years during the Holocaust.

None of them could leave the attic so the only thing Anne could do was write about everything that was going on in her surroundings. Anne wrote *"despite everything, I believe people are really good at heart."* This coming from a teenage girl whose freedom, dreams and hopes were ripped away in instant and yet she still chose to believe. I can't even begin to imagine if this happened to me and my family would I be able to have the same attitude as Anne? She is one of my role models. Her wisdom spoke volumes and yet she was never able to really see the outcome her writings. Anne passed away at the age of 15 due to a sickness called Typhus.

Though she left this earth at such a young age, The Diary of Anne Frank has been translated into 67 languages and has sold over 30 million copies. It was also the catalyst in which Erin Gruwell, in the movie *Freedom Writers,* would use to reach the hearts of her students. Anne Frank did not set out to become a famous writer. She just instinctively knew she had something to say and decided to write.

Is there a story you long to write? What is holding you back from either writing in a journal the way Anne did or just simply speaking up? You never know who is listening.

Did you know that even a whisper can be heard from ten miles away? If you were standing on the top of a mountain looking out on a gigantic piece of the earth in the darkness, you can see bright lights hundreds of miles away. In complete darkness, it is possible to see the flame of a candle flickering up to thirty miles away from you.

When I accepted the role of Eva in *Freedom Writers*, I was inspired as I learned the story of Erin Gruwell and her tenacious spirit. She had no idea that these kids were left to fend for themselves on the streets. When she saw them she could have simply felt sorry for them, but she didn't. She chose to teach them to see themselves as survivors instead of victims. Erin's perspective was much different from the other teachers and instead of seeing them as unteachable kids, she saw that they were diamonds in the rough who just needed some polishing. There is a lot of work that has to be done in *you* before you can change the world. God allowed me to play such an intense role, because He knew I had my own story to tell, and if it wasn't for *Freedom Writers* I truly believe I would have not had the courage to tell my story. This journey is not going to be an overnight change for you. It took me ten years of baby steps and crawling before I could even attempt to learn to walk again.

I had to figure out how I could use my situation to bless others. I had to learn how to take my pain to show purpose in someone else's world. Eva's fight and

pain gave me a purpose. You have to take a chance if you hope to change the world.
I dare you to be daring.

In 2015, I was given the opportunity to be a speaker at the women's conference at my church. I was beyond grateful for this moment because if there is one thing I live for it is empowering other women. My pastor asked me to share my story of being a survivor, so I stood in front of the church and told the story to a room full of over 700 women. After my session was over, a woman came up to me crying and thanking me for being brave enough to share my story. She was a survivor as well.

The woman explained to me she had high levels of anxiety and was on meds to cope with her emotions. "I have good days sometimes, but the bad days are really bad and intense. I am praying to God to help me through this because I don't want to be on pills for the rest of my life." She'd only been out of her relationship for about a year. I told her how long it would take to heal and that I was in no way fully recovered. It is a day by day process fighting those villains, and they always appear at the perfect times to remind you of your weaknesses and your faults. They never go away completely. I reassured her that it was okay to have bad days and embrace both and make sure to feel. You are going to have bad days. But the sun will rise tomorrow, I promise.

A few Sunday's later I saw her and she came walking up to me happily smiling. She proudly told me that she had just graduated from her domestic violence class. She was bright and beautiful and glowing and looked at me with so much hope as she said, "I know one day I will talk about my experience just like you."

Every time I see her, I can tell she is growing and changing for the better. I realized that I really could make a difference with just a few words.

I grabbed her and hugged her as I looked her in the eyes and said "I can't wait for the day to hear you speak."

That woman's message might be different than mine. Her story might be different. But the most important thing is that she found her voice again and it is being heard. You must realize the importance of your words. You might speak to someone somewhere, on a train, on a bus or in a park. It doesn't have to be a grand gesture; it can be a whisper. It can be a flicker of light. Someone will hear you. Someone will see you.

Every person has a story. Every person has a past. We are all trying to recover from what we feel our mistakes have been. Some mistakes are larger than others, some pain cuts deeper, some situations silence us. We can either choose to remain silent or share with the world our experiences. Your voice matters and you have to power to change the world.

Today is the day that you choose to be heard. It's time for you to make your mess into a message. Share your story with all of the ups and downs that go along with it. It's not going to be a fairy tale. It won't be perfect every time. You might look fear in the face and get dropped to the ground. You might fall back into old habits. But you are strong enough to come back from any event. Being a strong woman doesn't mean that you've always defeated the enemy. Being a strong woman means that you can stand back up after you've been knocked down, clear your throat and move forward!

Make Your Mess Into A Message
Your Voice, Your Choice

- How do you believe there are ways to make your mess into a message?

  _____

  _____

  _____

  _____

  _____

  _____

  _____

  _____

  _____

  _____

- What story do you have inside you that you have wanted to share?

  _____

  _____

  _____

  _____

  _____

  _____

  _____

  _____

  _____

  _____

  _____

  _____

Dream Big, Take Action

One of the greatest gifts my parents bestowed upon me as a child was the ability to dream big. I mean *really* big. From the first moment I can remember, all I would hear them tell me was that I could be anything I wanted to be; as long as I worked hard, got my education, dedicated myself and dreamt big. I still live by those principals and I have to say they were absolutely right. I know it may sound like a cliché; "Dream big," but I am a living proof dreams do come true.

You know how I know? Because this book is something I dreamt of over 15 years ago. Now, did I think my first book would be written about my abuse? Absolutely not, but I knew deep down in my soul that one day I would write a book. Do I dream of it being a New York Time's bestseller? Um, YES! Do I dream of winning an Oscar? Of course, what actor doesn't? But if I don't try, then how will I ever know if it's possible? This chapter is about you and your dreams and understanding how precious they are to us as individuals. It is time to stop doubting and questioning every part of your life. You are enough. I will say that again. YOU ARE ENOUGH. You have everything inside of you to begin your journey towards making your dreams come true. I want to challenge you to think outside of the box of your world and make a choice to really live the life you were created for. The great Maya Angelou once wrote, "*A person is the product of their dreams. So make sure to dream great dreams. And then try to live your dream.*"

As I began my own journey towards hope and putting the pieces back together after my abusive relationship, I will admit it was definitely a struggle. Now that I was free from the situation and trying to move on, I still felt frozen. I had trouble finding the motivation to actually *move*. But the one thing that did help me find hope again was all of the dreams I still had living inside of me. Even after all the beatings I endured, it was as if God protected my dreams from going down the drain. It made me realize, as much as my abuser did his best to control me with fear and violence, in the end he never took my dreams from me. Your dreams belong to you and no one else. My parents had done such a wonderful job of instilling those principals inside of me at such a young age, that even after all of the blood and pain, they lingered, like the smell of my mother's cooking or my father's cologne. Even through all the darkness, I could still hear my father's voice telling me that I was beautiful and nothing was impossible if I believed. It was the voice of my biological father, but it was also the voice of my heavenly father. Even when I wanted to die, I still had those dreams, those words inside of me.

My dreams saved me from myself.

But dreaming wasn't enough for me.

Allow me to ask you this question: What is the difference between you and Oprah? Take a moment to think about it. Don't worry, I'll wait. If you have a piece of paper next to you or your phone has a notepad, I want you to write down your answer. Now that you have written your answer down I will take a guess at some of the things you might have come up, ok? So let us begin. Some of us might say, Oprah is a billionaire. She created her network (OWN). She has the resources to make not only her dreams come true, but many people's dreams come true. Oprah has access to prominent people and celebrities. Oprah has her magazine called, O. And one more thing; she founded an all-girls school in Africa. Am I on the right track? Ok good. Now you may be thinking, "Ok April, where are you going with this?"

Well, what you might not know about Oprah is from at the age of 9, she was raped. Then from the ages of 10 to 14 she was sexually abused by family members. At the age of fourteen, she became pregnant and within a few weeks the baby passed away. But something incredible happened to her after the loss of the baby. When she went to go live with her father, Oprah said in an interview with Barbara Walters, "my father looked at me and said 'You have a second chance at life." Oprah understood in that crucial moment that her life was not ending but it was just beginning. Her perspective on the situation had shifted in a way that led her to begin dreaming beyond the circumstances surrounding her. So, is there really a difference between you and Oprah? I personally don't see a difference. At the end of the day she is a human being just like you and I. Oprah experienced extreme hardship and yet made a powerful choice to move forward in her life.

Have you ever said to yourself, "If only I had enough time and money I would pursue my dreams." Maybe you even have thought, "Why bother dreaming if my situation is never going to change anyway?" I confess, I have said these words many times in my life. And nothing positive has ever come from what Joyce Meyer calls "stinkin thinkin". The only thing holding you back from your dreams and goals is you!

But April, *"You don't know my story; you have no idea what I have experienced how dare you ask me to dream when I can barely think straight."* I hear you, believe me I do, but courage doesn't come from what you can do it comes from what you can't do. Not only am I asking you to dream bigger, I am daring you to take action! I should be six feet under-ground right now because of my abuse but I am not. And because I know there are millions of people who will never get the opportunity to speak up, I will you my voice for them as long as I can breathe.

In my home, my husband and I have a rule and it is this: *If you come with a complaint but you have no solution then you are part of the problem. The only way you are allowed to complain is if you have a solution.*

I really don't do well with people who are complainers so please pray for me! Why do I mention this? Because in order for you to make your dreams a reality you MUST TAKE ACTION! I had to put that in caps just to make sure you got my point. So April how do I take action? Well, I am so happy you asked. Allow me to introduce to you three tactics I have personally used in order to be a woman of action.

Write Your Vision

When I was in middle school I would write my name all over my notebook and add stars next to it. I guess you can say I was subconsciously speaking life into my destiny. I can't say I wanted to be famous at that point, but something inside of me knew I wanted to make an impact on the world. It was my autograph that allowed me to dream and feel something bigger than me. I would write down all of my goals and dreams every chance I could. I have the journals to prove it. As I mentioned in prior chapters, my reality while growing up during the crack epidemic era didn't seem to bright, but I knew I had to get out; and with no one really telling me to do it, I just wrote out what I wanted to see happen in my future.

In the book of Habakkuk 2:2 (NIV) it reads, "Then the Lord replied: Write down the revelation and make it plain on tablets so that a herald may run with it."

When I read this verse it made my heart fill up with joy, because it was confirming what I have done for so many years and what many successful people do- they write down their vision. This isn't rocket science nor do I take credit for it at all, but it works. How many times have you come up with so many great ideas and nothing ever comes of it? Just imagine if Shakespeare would have never written down his beautiful sonnets and plays. We would have been deprived of works like Romeo and Juliet, Hamlet and Macbeth, just to name a few.

But April I don't have time to write. Yes you do! If you have time to go on social media to check to see if someone liked another selfie that you took, then you have time to write down what you want to see for your future! And when you are writing it down, make sure that you are specific. For example, if you are trying to lose weight, don't just write down "I want to lose ten pounds." Write down how you plan to reach your goal. How many times will you work out? What kind of eating plan will you create? Do you have an accountability partner? When you are specific with what you want to achieve, then you become more aware of the things that may distract you. Write the vision down. Be specific.

For this book I had to write down an outline of my chapters and a paragraph after the title describing what each one was about. Because I was very specific when I began to write the book, it made the writing process easier and my thoughts were not fragmented and in disarray.

That leads me into my next point.

Build A Circle of Influence (C.O.I)

During my abusive relationship there were times I felt very lonely, because my ex- boyfriend used tactics to keep me isolated from my friends and family. For instance, if we would make plans to go out for a night, right before we would leave he would start an argument for no reason, and I would end up cancelling on my friends. Eventually they stopped calling me and I don't blame them because they were unaware of the situation.

What I was not aware of, was that in order for my healing process to begin after the relationship I had to surround myself with goal oriented people. I knew if I wanted to become a successful person I could not do it on my own. Unfortunately, many women find themselves raising a family on their own and some men as well, so it feels as though they have to do everything by themselves. I am sure you have heard the phrase "if you want to get something done you have to do it yourself." As much as this statement runs true, and I have felt many times like I had to do things on my own, I know without a doubt I cannot achieve greatness alone. Your circle of influence is absolutely important in your journey towards taking action towards your future. What does this mean? The people who you have in your life right now, the people who influence your decisions, people who you seek advice from, people who push you to be great at what you do, those people are your circle of influence.

We live in a society today where friendships have become very shallow due to the new ways of communication via social media. Back in my day, we had to call everyone on the phone or send letters to one another which made things much more personal. But today if you don't really feel like talking to someone you can just text and that's pretty much it. We have become more accustomed to how many people are following us instead of creating real authentic relationships. I can count the friends I have on one hand (which is sometimes sad but also very strategic), because each of those persons adds value to whom I am as an individual. I know I can seek wisdom from people who live their lives with integrity and character.

My father would always tell me, "you will be judged by the friends you keep." As much as we dislike the word "judge," in the end it is very true. If you are a parent and your child begins to hang around people who are not into the most positive activities, oh believe me you will definitely make your opinion known to your child to be aware of the friends they keep. As we become adults we should maintain that same mindset. If you want to go to a mountain top and the person you share this with has never even seen a mountain, then how can they lead you there? When I was getting ready to go into high school, I remember I was so nervous and scared of not being liked or fitting in.

My brother looked at me and said, "April if you want to be smart, hang out with smart people."

So I did just that and I succeeded in being an "A" student because I connected with people who were smarter than me in the areas where I was weak. I am horrible at math. As a matter of fact, I still count on my fingers, so I stayed after school and worked in math groups in order to pass the class. I did what I had to do in order to succeed!

I would like for you to take a moment. Go ahead, I'll wait. Great, now I want you to really think about your circle of influence. Who do you have in your life right now, that you can dream with? Who in your life challenges you to be the best you? Who can be honest with you when they need to be and you not get offended? Who in your life makes you think outside the box? This is really important because in order for you to reach your destiny and take action you cannot do it alone. If you could not come up with anyone, that is ok. Make a list of people that you would like to start surrounding yourself with. Who do you aspire to be like?

When Oprah saw Barbara Walters on television it gave her the hope that she too could one day be a television journalist. I remember the first time I saw Jennifer Lopez dancing on, *In Living Color* and I couldn't stop smiling, and especially when I found out she was from the Bronx and Puerto Rican. I almost died and went to heaven. Never in my life did I see someone who looked like me, came from the same place as me (the Bronx), and had the same ethnic background on television. I knew at that moment anything was possible! Sometimes we have to be the first ones to do something to break the cycle; like being the first in your family to graduate from college. For most people, this is one of the biggest dreams to ever come true. Because you are not only doing it for you; you're doing it for your family and the generations to come. Dream Big. Take Action.

So far I have shared with you that in order to dream big and take action you must write down your vision and be specific. Surround yourself with a strong circle of influence because those are the people who will help you in reaching your destiny. Now, this last one is definitely a key point towards reaching your full potential. Are you ready? I hope you are.

Believe in the Possible
"Oh April I hear this all time. How do you expect me to believe when everything in my world is telling me not to?"

This is how I expect you to. If you woke up today and could take a breath, then it means you are alive. If you are alive, it tells me you have the power to change your mind no matter what, only if you want it that bad. So, how bad do you want it? It is time to stop all the excuses and take responsibility for your dreams. Will you want to quit? Absolutely. Does life suck sometimes and isn't fair? Yes. But if you are tired of being sick and tired of your situation then this last paragraph is for you.

I told you I don't do well with people who complain about everything. If you are not a person seeking solutions, then this chapter isn't for you. Sorry if I may sound harsh, but sometimes it is necessary we hear the truth. It can hurt to hear the truth, but it can also set us free. Can I get an, amen?

Sometime during this life we will experience things that just seem completely unfair. There are some people who appear to live life with really no problems or "drama" is how I like to call it. Then there are those who experience such traumatic situations that I can't even bear to think of. If you turn on the news for more than five minutes, you see so many horrific stories it makes you reexamine your life and realize, "Hey, my life is not that bad."

When I think of my abuse, I think to myself, "How did I ever make it out alive?" Then I listen to other stories of women who are survivors and some of these stories make me think, "How did they ever get out of the situation?" I remember hearing about a woman's husband who sliced her arm open with a knife and then put crazy glue on it to try to close the wound. There was another story of a woman who was raped by her father starting at the age of two. I truly believe there is real evil in the world. But what comforts me is when I read the verse in Mark 9:23 (NIV) where Jesus says, "Everything is possible for those who believe." Even if you have the faith of a mustard seed, which one grain is about 1 to 2 millimeters in size, you have to power to change.

One of my favorite movies of all time is Rocky. As a matter of fact, all of the Rocky movies are my favorites. But the last film, Rocky Balboa, was full of great screenwriting and the dialogue was so honest and truthful. Rocky and his son are having a conversation and his son is basically asking his father to not go through with his upcoming fight. Rocky responds with one of the greatest monologues written for the screen. He says, "It *ain't about how hard you hit: it's about hard you can get hit and keep moving forward. It's how much you can take and keep moving forward. That's how winning is done."* There is more to the speech but I picked this piece because it really hit home for me. Abuse can literally destroy all your dreams. It can knock the wind out of your soul. Life itself can seem so hard to believe in anything; let alone yourself.

But I believe in you.

I may never meet you. We may never cross paths but I believe in you because someone believed in me. And if you picked up this book and made it to the last chapter, would you be willing to go a little further? I am not asking you to do anything against your will. I am in no way pushing my beliefs onto you. What I have shared in my book is what has helped me along my journey. It's not about what faith you believe in or what is your sexual orientation. I am not interested in any of that. All I am asking from you is to begin right at this moment believing you deserve better in life.

You will be the first to graduate college. You will find love. You will have the family you always wanted. You will get out of debt. You will become a person of integrity. You will become the person you always dreamed of becoming. You will heal from your pain. You will have a vision for your life. You will have a circle of influence that wants you to succeed. You have the power to change. Your voice matters. You matter…

#Dream Big. Be Bold. Take Action...

Dream Big, Take Action
Your Voice, Your Choice

- What is your vision for your future? Take action! Write the vision down. Write down what your dream is no matter how big or how small and look at those words every chance that you get.

  _____

  _____

  _____

  _____

  _____

  _____

  _____

  _____

  _____

- Write down three people in your life who are in your circle of influence.

  _____

  _____

  _____

- Write down in a few words what you believe about yourself. Who believes in you? What you believe for the future?

  _____

  _____

  _____

  _____

Resources

If you or someone you know has been in an abusive relationship, there are many different resources to assist you in your journey towards healing and recovery.

National Domestic Violence Hotline
1 (800) 799-7233
www.thehotline.org

National Coalition Against Domestic Violence
www.ncadv.org

Center Against Domestic Violence
www.cadvny.org

Connect Training Institute
www.connectnyc.org

Anti-Violence Project
(212) 714-1141
www.avp.org LGBTQ community

Children's Aid Society
(212) 503-6842
www.childrensaidsociety.org

The Healing Center
(718) 238-5138
www.thehealingcenterny.org

No More
www.nomore.org

Break The Cycle
www.Breakthecycle.org

Love Is Respect
www.loveisrespect.org

Safe Horizon
www.safehorizon.org

Casa De Esperanza
www.Casadeesperanza.org

Acknowledgements

God without your love, grace, and endless mercy I would not have made it through some of the toughest storms. Every time I felt like giving up you pursued me and sent people to lift me up and pray for me. I can never thank you enough.

Mom- thank you for teaching me one of the greatest lessons that I plan on passing onto Summer Rose-her voice matters. Daddy, what can I say you are my hero, no matter how bad things may seem your smile, enthusiasm, and phone calls always keep me going!

To my entire family thank you for supporting me in this special time with your patience, love, and support. I could not do any of this without you all.

To my mother in law Rosa, thank you so much for watching after Summer Rose while I took time to write. Thank you for all you love, support, and prayer.

To my Connect Institute Family- you have not only equipped me with the tools to really understand Intimate Partner Violence, but have given me so much love and room to grow as a woman. You are a huge part of my life and I will forever be grateful..

Rita Smith- you are a force of nature! No one sees the work you do behind closed doors and all that you give. I thank you from the bottom of my heart and soul for doing the work.

Rhonda, the moment we spoke on the phone over five years ago it was an instant connection. We have listened to each other's stories, cried a few times, and pushed each other to continue growing. This book is for you...

Toni Ellis, sister every time I speak to you I feel like I can conquer the world. You spark my soul with encouragement and love...Now can we write a book together? lol...

Danielle, my best friend, thank you for your loyalty, confidence, love, and respect. Our friendship is like a vintage bottle of wine-better and more fabulous with age!

Tina- You are such an inspiration to me and your food heals my soul. You are courageous beyond measure. I love you so much thank you...

Q- You played such an important role in my life. No matter what has happened between us your friendship molded me in so many ways.

Erika Alexander- The moment we met at Sundance we instantly connected! We realized we were both two ladies who were not afraid to voice our opinions. I love you and so proud of you and Tony for making your dreams a reality. I will never forget what you guys did for me in Lala land...

Eric Metaxas- Who would have thought our worlds would collide and we would actually become friends. Thank you for writing the foreword. I will never forget the day I made you laugh it boosted my confidence! Thank you for your intelligence and witty humor but also for your love for our Savior...

Rebecca thank you for encouraging me when the writing was too much to bare at times.

Words of Life- Pastor Ben and Pastor Tere you both have played crucial roles in my journey as a believer. Thank you for setting such high standards and pushing me to dream bigger than ever. Thank you to all the prayer warriors who lift me up even when I am unaware. You know who you are...

Dr. Rev. Alfred Correa and Marilyn- thank you both for allowing me to process some of the most difficult moments in my life with you. The amount of knowledge and education I acquired in our time together has no price tag. I will always have an attitude of gratitude.

To my nieces Destini, Precious, and Krystal you were wonderfully and fearfully made! Always remember to be yourselves!

To J.W. Cortes and Victor Cruz, we have had countless conversations about our dreams and to have you both be part of this journey means the world to me and Jose. I can never repay you both for pushing me to believe in myself and my writing. Thank you.

Gina Rugolo- What can I say I love you! No matter how things have turned out you kept believing. I can't wait till we win an Oscar and enjoy our traditional meal- In and Out burgers.

Cool Speak...Carlos, Ernesto, and Joey I have never been more challenged to grow in my life than since the day I signed with the company. Carlos, words cannot not even be put together to say how grateful I am for you and your family. You kept pushing me to write and for a while I just kept holding off but here we are publishing my first book. Other than having my daughter this is the hardest and scariest thing I have ever done in my life. We are both immense dreamers so it's great to dream with someone who is crazier than me! Ernesto aka (Lt. Dan) you challenge me to be the best and the fact I get to learn from someone like you is just priceless. Joey you are the calm before the storm thank you for being so positive about everything!

To my husband Jose…I have said this before and I will say it again your love saved me from myself. After the abuse I really did not think I could ever find true love and God had it all worked out when we fell in love over fifteen years ago. Your patience healed my soul, your gentleness made me feel safe, and your selflessness taught me how to give. This book could not even exist if it weren't for you believing in me and allowing me the time to write. I love you now more than ever…I am your wife now and forever.

To Summer Rose, I hope when you read this book in a couple of years you can understand who your mommy was in the past and how she did her best to turn her life around. I will never lie to you about my life. I just pray you are inspired to become a woman of boldness, love, compassion and someone who fights for the rights of others. Mommy loves you more than you can ever know…

About the Author

April Hernandez Castillo is an actor, motivational speaker, survivor, TV host, and SAG nominee. April resides in New York City with her husband Jose T. Castillo Jr., and their three-year-old daughter Summer Rose and toy dog, Bambi. April and Jose have their own film company, LionChaser Films. They seek to create purposeful content to encourage, educate, and empower the masses. One of her dreams is to hold a women's conference in Yankee Stadium one day. April loves to workout, drink tea, and take long walks with her husband...

Made in the USA
Columbia, SC
18 April 2018